KICK IT!

The Definitive Football Mixtape

Paul Brand

Published by Halcyon Publishing

First published 2024

Cover design: Steve Leard
Layout: Rob MacDonald
Edited by Adam Bushby & Rob MacDonald

Printed & bound by:
Ashford Colour Press
Unit 220, Fareham Reach,
Fareham Road, Gosport,
Hampshire PO13 0FW

"The British are among the worst idlers in the world ... Indian children aspire to be doctors ... the British are more interested in football and pop music."

Britannia Unchained, co-authored by former British Prime Minister Liz Truss

To 13-year-old me, who thought it a good idea to buy a cassette version of Status Quo and Manchester United for a friend. Rest assured, tastes will improve and you will find other friends.

Also to Vicky, James and Daisy for putting up with my dual obsessions.

About the author

Football and writing have long gone hand-in-hand for Paul, who first developed a passion for prose in a player-reporter role for his free-scoring primary school team. For more than three decades it looked as if he'd peaked early, the standard publishing rejections punctuating careers in music administration and teaching, while his Sunday League endeavours were best described as ordinary.

He now pays the bills by creating learning resources to help overworked teachers educate the next generation, but he'd rather be writing about important stuff like football, music and film, and was therefore celebrating like Roger Milla when his first book was published in 2023. This is his hat-trick effort.

Track listing

Liner notes

Enjoy the silence? Not at the football. Stadia and fanbases are frequently judged by the volume of noise generated, and the lockdown conditions of the 2019-20 and 2020-21 seasons provided an eerie insight into what sport is like without the sound of the crowd.

Interestingly, many grounds continued to pump out music, greeting the players as they entered the arena and celebrating goals scored or wins notched. Behind closed doors, with no-one but the playing, coaching, medical and media staff present, the diegetic participants would have been hyper-aware of the artificiality of piped music, especially when met with silence bar their own shouts. So why persist with audio transmissions to an empty stadium? The answer lies in part in the symbiotic relationship between the industries of football and music, with clubs continuing to replicate the 'match-day experience' for a virtual crowd, spectating via their television sets. Moreover, we also have to acknowledge that football has long since gone 'meta' and many now watch from their living rooms — the game is part of the global entertainment business as much as a grassroots sport and leisure pastime.

One of the other peculiarities of Covid-era football was the participants being more clearly audible without the crowd noise drowning them out. While communication is important on the pitch, and ever more important off it as well, conventional wisdom has it that footballers are better at expressing themselves with their feet than with their voices. Andy Fletcher, keyboardist with Depeche Mode, told *FourFourTwo* in 2001: "When I meet footballers I'm so over-awed because they can do things that I could never do." However, the other side have not always been so respectful of the football-music skills delineation. And it's partly the fans' fault for encouraging them ...

Why do we sing?

Any attempt at understanding the alliance between football and music must venture back at least a century. In his 2014 article '"See, the Conquering Hero Comes! Sound the Trumpets, Beat the Drums": Music and Sport in England, 1880-1939', Professor Dave Russell argues that both before and after the First World War, sports fans "maintained vigorous music-making traditions of their own, a logical extension of the habits of singing and playing in the street, the public house and other locations that were such a common feature of social life in the period".

Many of the Football League's founding clubs were upshots of industrialisation (midland and northern factory and mill towns dominated) and it has been argued that sports fans of the 19th century, displaced from traditional rural communities, were seeking a new sense of identity. Eric Hobsbawm, British historian and expert on the rise of capitalism, socialism and nationalism, noted that football quickly became a transmitter of national as well as regional identity, explaining that "the imagined community of millions seems more real as a team of 11 named people".

In an article that appeared in the *Daily Gazette for Middlesbrough* on 7 December 1889, the correspondent summed it up thus:

> "A football match simply seems to be a sort of popular safety valve for the pent-up energies and passions of an energetic and high-spirited people. The roar of the football crowd is raised in one long continued roar of request, command, entreaty and reproach and the most phlegmatic of men finds himself carried away by the exhilarating influences of the mimic war."

Singing and chanting was already part of the cacophony. In a similar article that appeared in the *Belfast News Letter* in December 1898, under the heading 'Amusements Football Crowds Invent', it was reported that, "Every big club has its own particular song and by singing this the spectators can keep themselves in good humour."

Newspaper reports of the same period confirm that the Southampton 'Whisper' could be heard at the stadium and at places where fans congregated before and after a match. This ironically titled war cry was a rhythmic 'Yi! Yi! Yi!' that escalated in volume and had an equivalent that emanated from Third Lanark Athletic Club in Glasgow. The locations are significant because their port industries indicate a means of cultural transmission.

Sailing ahead to the 20th century, advances in transportation and technology sped up this transmission. Fast-forward to the 21st century and songs such as 'Allez, Allez, Allez' (which went from Serie D to Champions League via Italy, Spain, Portugal, Scotland and Liverpool) can go global almost instantaneously thanks to the viral spread of social media. Across centuries, the impulse is the same and is exactly what led folk musician Martin Carthy to say that "football crowds represent the one true surviving embodiment of an organic living folk tradition", by which he means that there is an intrinsic urge to take a tune, adapt it to a new communal purpose and then pass it on. Christopher Morley, writing in an article titled 'Singing in the Stands' (2014), followed the thread back to the Stone Age:

> "Next time you take your seat, just listen, safe in the knowledge you're most definitely part of something, carrying on a tradition that may well be generations old ... A sort of extension of the caveman's 'battle trance' state which is considered by many the root of all human music, encouraging groups to stick together, pull through and stave off predators by sheer will."

Singing is proven to release endorphins, serotonin and dopamine — the brain's feel-good chemicals and hormones — but the importance of the communal, ritualistic elements explains why spectators will happily hurl invective at Sky Sports, but rarely tune up their voices to break into solo song in front of their home entertainment systems.

So, physiology, psychology and sociology can explain why supporters like a good old sing-song. What it doesn't explain so well is why footballers themselves think it a good idea to augment the hum from the terraces by recording new songs for them to sing?

Why do they sing (or not, nowadays)?

In *The People's Songs: The Story of Modern Britain in 50 Records* (2013), the radio DJ and music critic Stuart Maconie points out that the pastimes and professions of football and music have much in common:

> "Both are essentially working-class pursuits that have gained a huge international audience, and both have offered social mobility to young people, mainly men, from industrial and post-industrial urban communities. Both depend on the passionate commitment and enthusiasm of a dedicated consumer who will spend money and time following their favourite artist, band or team."

That last part about the 'dedicated consumer' helps explain why footballers first went into the recording studio: their employers sought to monetise brand loyalty, and the working-class players were perfectly game, as were fans hitherto starved of ways to display their tribal allegiance outside of match days; replica kits, for example, were first produced in the 1950s but it was only in the 1970s that their commercial appeal became apparent.

The explosion in football songs coincided with the post-war technological revolution, when mass ownership of media devices such as the wireless, combined with affordable international travel, meant new means of cultural transmission, as identified by zoologist Desmond Morris in *The Soccer Tribe* (1981). Morris detected a shift from the Victorian community hymn-singing before sporting events (exemplified by the endurance of 'Abide with Me', which has preceded every FA Cup Final since 1927) to a new era of pop, in which DJs rather than conductors became the tastemakers, and the transference from sheet music to vinyl placed music in the hands of the proletariat.

By the 1970s, British Rail had begun running the League Liner, a cheap rail service for travelling football fans famously containing a disco carriage. Guinness World Records' *British Hit Singles and Albums* chronicles 43 different single releases by the various clubs and international football associations across the last three decades of the 20th century, plus many more unofficial releases and solo efforts from player-cum-pop-stars.

Since the turn of the millennium, enthusiasm has waned. Only those for whom it was a novel experience bothered to commemorate a cup run ('Yeovil True' and 'Oh Millwall' in 2004; Cardiff's 'Bluebirds Flying High' in 2008), while Fabio Capello banned the remnants of England's 'Golden Generation' from entering the recording studio, as well as from eating ketchup and butter, a sure tell-tale sign that the link between football and blue-collar society was broken. Players still date pop stars but it is crass to want to be one in an age when recording royalties pale in comparison to footballers' wages. Million-pound endorsements would more likely be endangered than advanced by a player warming up their vocals, although singing remains a favourite locker-room initiation ceremony and some use TikTok (formerly musical.ly) to build individual brand identities.

At the same time that football clubs have morphed from playgrounds for men who perhaps should have known better into slick business operations, the music industry has suffered an existential crisis. Digitalisation was supposed to democratise music commerce but has instead handed power to the robotic overlords of streaming platforms. Just as crucially, the value of the "passionate commitment and enthusiasm of a dedicated consumer", as cited by Maconie, has evaporated; streaming has made casuals the kingmakers — fans who are heavily invested in their favourite artists now make little more difference to their success than someone who picks a ready-made playlist as background music. Football fans who feel like faceless consumers, detached from their clubs and powerless to impact on boardroom takeovers, can probably relate. Thanks to the gloss of Premier League marketing, football has overtaken music as the dominant (read lucrative) entertainment industry, so that we have an inverse synergy from the heyday of the football-music crossover: now, rather than footballers miming on *Top of the Pops*, we have entertainers lacing up their boots for the annually televised Soccer Aid, set up by wannabe footballers Robbie Williams and Jonathan Wilkes in 2006. And in keeping with the modern 'football as business' credo, Ed Sheeran and Jake Bugg have opted to sponsor Ipswich Town and Notts County, respectively, rather than penning odes to their hometown teams.

It is a paradox then that, as the sport has become increasingly commercialised, the official single (or, in more ambitious cases, album) has died a death. And with the music industry ever more fragmented, you'd think that captive audiences with a global reach would appeal to beleaguered label bosses as well as stars-in-their-eyes club owners. Wolverhampton Wanderers recognised the crossover appeal when launching Wolves Records in 2021, lauded (by themselves) as "an ambitious and unique proposition that will unite two of the world's biggest passions ... [and] see performing artists benefit from the reach of a Premier League football club's global audience while also gaining access to ADA's [partner

Warner Music's Alternative Distribution Alliance] marketing and distribution expertise". It didn't include Conor Coady being offered a recording contract, and the label's signings have thus far proven less successful even than Fabio Silva or Gonçalo Guedes.

What makes a good football song?

Ask a member of Generation Z, born after the release of 'Three Lions', to name a good football song and they're as likely to nominate Glass Animals' 'Heat Waves', identified by a 2022 study as the most popular song from the FIFA video game franchise, as they are 'Back Home' or 'When the Saints Go Marching In'. Sky Sports has embossed Republica's 'Ready to Go' and Celeste's 'Stop This Flame' as 'football songs', even though they could just as easily have been licensed for motor racing, cricket or snooker. Then again, the links between the beautiful game and some of the music hall staples covered in the pages that follow are equally tenuous.

The contents of this book are concerned with the intersection of the football and music industries, with the focus on charts rather than chants, the latter of which typically has more in common with satirical British humour than with professional music. In the grand folk tradition, many of the best chants are re-versions of traditional tunes or classic pop songs — the Beach Boys' 'Sloop John B.' is the basis of a myriad of chants but the composers (Brian Wilson adapted a Bahamian folk song previously credited to Carl Sandburg) don't collect royalties for the terrace covers, even though football stadiums are licensed by the Performing Rights Society and Phonographic Performance Ltd, the UK bodies responsible for making sure musicians are remunerated for use of their work. Chants are mostly ephemeral. The records played by the stadium DJs can be more easily inventoried and do provide a royalty income stream, however meagre. The songs included here have either stood the test of time or specifically commemorated a memorable sporting event, paying out handsomely to their rights holders.

Which is not to say that they're all quality records and worthy members of the canon. The football song is a novelty genre that invites plenty of ridicule, akin to Eurovision (with which it has a surprisingly strong correlation). But, like its camp intercontinental cousin, its lack of cool is all part of the charm, included in which is a nostalgia for the days when football was first and foremost a game or, at the serious end, a lifestyle rather than a business. At their best, our club anthems and international hits tap into the communal identity, experience and passion that have been shown to be powerful contributors to why sports fans sing as one.

Even the very best, however, would struggle to stake a claim to being works of art. They are more like nursery rhymes, which is not to diminish their power or significance. Typically, a football song should be easy to sing, often abridged to the chorus only, with obliquely relevant lyrics. More 'We Are the Champions' than 'Bohemian Rhapsody'. Famously, EMI were reluctant to release Queen's genre-splicing masterpiece and the one thing it does have in common with the average football song is that, tour de force or trash, there's little explanation for why they strike a chord with the man in the street.

There's a certain amount of serendipity behind the success of most anthems: right time, right place. Dementia studies show that music has an unparalleled ability to connect to time and place, and football songs derive a great deal of potency from defining a moment. Which is probably the main reason why their potency can't be bottled and reproduced. One dismal attempt to manufacture atmosphere was the 2004 Barclays Premiership Chant Laureate competition, endorsed by Poet Laureate Andrew Motion and won by Jonny Hurst, a Birmingham fan who inexplicably crossed tribal lines and waxed lyrical about Aston Villa striker Juan Pablo Ángel. The evaluation of Colin Irwin, one-time assistant editor of *Melody Maker* and supporter of Woking FC, was more unerring: "There's one thing this [competition] proves; terrace anthems can't be artificially inseminated, they evolve naturally from genuine fans drawing on the passion, identity, adrenalin, comradeship, excitement and atmosphere of the moment."

There is evidence from as early as 1906 that local newspapers and match programmes encouraged supporters to submit their own verse in the hope that it would ignite the crowd; officially sanctioned songs are an extension of a tradition that also included the employment of pre-match marching bands to liven things up. In an era of inflated prices that have devastated football's working-class soul and ushered in the 'prawn-sandwich brigade', it is notable that many stadiums are turning to designated singing sections in an effort to combat sterility. The bell appears to have tolled on the football song as record/cassette/CD/MP3 (only two of our entries date from this century), but while there's breath in the crowd, there's hope of a comeback ...

The Definitive Football Mixtape(s)

If you'd like to support the talented (and not-so-talented) creators of our mixtape audio content, then you can listen to ready-made playlists while you read, earning them royalties to the tune of approximately £0.002 per stream ...

Spotify search terms:

- Kick It
- Kick It — Alternative Mix
- Kick It — Bonus Tracks

by paulbrand

Side A: Club Anthems

1. You'll Never Walk Alone

First released: 1945
Highest UK chart position: 1

How did a Rodgers and Hammerstein show tune weave its way into the hearts of working-class football supporters on the other side of the Atlantic? What exactly was the route from Broadway via Hollywood to Anfield?

There are no explicit pointers in the plot of *Carousel*, the show for which it was written. The story of carnival barker Billy Bigelow and mill worker Julie Jordan contains no kickabouts and no epic sporting scenes. It does, however, contain the sort of heartrending emotion and drama that football followers might associate with penalty shootout agony. The song's narrative function is consolatory, crooned by Nettie Fowler — the cousin of Julie — to comfort the female lead after her errant husband Billy has died in her arms following a botched robbery. It is also achingly sentimental: it is given a reprise in the final scene as the ghost of Billy — granted permission to return to Earth for one day to make amends to his widow — watches the graduation class of Louise, the troubled daughter he never met.

Maudlin and born of misconduct, modern-day trolls might say it was perfectly suited to Scousers from the get-go. So it comes as a surprise to learn that the song's title could very easily have been inscribed on the gates of Old Trafford instead of Anfield.

The visit of Sheffield Wednesday for an FA Cup fifth-round tie on 15 February 1958 was the first match Manchester United played following the Munich air disaster nine days earlier. With 20 dead on impact, including seven players, and many others including manager Matt Busby still in hospital (where the future knight was twice read the Last Rites), the atmosphere was understandably sombre. The programme was left blank where the line-up should have been, a gesture heavy in symbolism but also compelled by necessity. A scratch team of youngsters, reserves and loanees — anchored by Harry Gregg and Bill Foulkes, the only survivors fit to play — somehow won 3-0. Prior to kick-off, members of the New Mills Operatic Society performed 'You'll Never Walk Alone', a song they had been rehearsing at the time of the crash, in tribute to the Busby Babes. It was seen as a fitting choice by the 60,000 in attendance, who joined in en masse to make for a rousing and tear-jerking rendition.

Indeed, some of those there that day claim their north-west rivals stole the song from them, although there is no evidence that it subsequently became a fixture on the Stretford End. And setting rivalry aside, Liverpool (for whom Busby had played for five years until war service intervened) offered five players on loan to help Manchester United fulfil their fixtures for the 1957-58 season, when there was a real chance of the club folding in the shadow of the tragedy. Given that such a poignant season ended at Wembley, as FA Cup runners-up, the idea of walking on through a storm resonates incredibly strongly, so perhaps the bigger surprise is that the reds of Manchester didn't persevere with *Carousel*'s defining number and it instead swung to the reds of Liverpool five years later.

So what instigated this move along the M62, which conveniently opened during the intermission? The answer is as prosaic as a cover version by Gerry and the Pacemakers.

The song was already widely known; as well as the 1956 film version of *Carousel*, recordings by Frank Sinatra, Judy Garland, Mario Lanza and Gene Vincent, among many others, had brought it to global attention. But it was Gerry Marsden's Merseybeat combo who first took it into the higher reaches of the UK pop charts.

Liverpool were one of the first clubs to employ a DJ, who would count down the top ten in the build-up to home matches. It is therefore reckoned that 'You'll Never Walk Alone' first reverberated around Anfield for the visit of West Bromwich Albion on 19 October 1963, when it entered the top ten at number seven. By the time Leicester came to Anfield two weeks later, it was at number one, meaning it was played on the public address system just before kick-off. Never mind that Liverpool lost 1-0, with match reports describing a bad-tempered affair that "the crowd of 47,438 did not like one little bit", the song at least was well received. When it was knocked off the top spot after four weeks (succeeded by the Beatles' 'She Loves You', the Fab Four's first single to top both the UK and US charts) and eventually dropped out of the top 10, Liverpudlians demanded that *their* song continue to be played.

While the moptops were busy invading the US, Liverpool fans had also taken an American standard and made it their own. Paul Du Noyer — author of a musical history of his home city, *Liverpool: Wondrous Place* — explains the sense of identity conferred by the success of Gerry and the Pacemakers' single:

> "There is a great solidarity in Liverpool and that is a virtue to which that song appeals ... People in Liverpool do feel that they are stuck on the edge of the land and when they gather in large numbers, whether it is at Anfield or Goodison, they do feel a sense of kinship that kicks in and the song is very effective at speaking to that feeling."

On-pitch success undoubtedly helped. The trophy-laden era of Bill Shankly doesn't dovetail neatly with the song's thematic concerns of despair and endurance, but the Merseybeat connection overrides such qualms. And prior to the golden sky of the 1960s, Shankly had delivered the club from relative gloom. Having spent most of the Fifties languishing in the Second Division, the Swinging Sixties represented a bright new era for the city both musically and in sport. In his 1968 book *The Football Man*, Arthur Hopcraft noted that the era brought "rehearsed chants and verses ... created in Liverpool, where the city character, with its pervading harshness of waterfront life, and bitterly combative Irish exile content, was given a sudden flowering of arrogant expression with the simultaneous rise of its pop musicians and of both its leading football teams."

The season that Gerry and the Pacemakers topped the charts, Liverpool were also crowned champions, having clambered out of Division Two only a couple of years earlier. This was a city very much in the ascendancy. They would claim a seventh league title in 1965-66. In between times, they would also lift the FA Cup for the first time. Indeed, when fans at Wembley for the 1965 Cup Final struck up a chorus of 'You'll Never Walk Alone' — taking the opportunity spurned by their Mancunian counterparts in 1958 to bind song and club in the national consciousness — TV commentator Kenneth Wolstenholme declared it their "signature song".

The identity of the modern Liverpool was being moulded; 1964 was also the year that the team switched to an all-red kit, as well as making their first foray into Europe. But it was in New York that the Pacemakers and the players came face to face. When Marsden realised that an appearance on *The Ed Sullivan Show* coincided with the team being in town for a pre-season tour, he convinced the programme's producers to invite them on as well. After the full team had joined the band on stage to perform 'You'll Never Walk Alone', Shankly approached the lead singer and said: "Gerry, my son, I have given you a football team and you have given us a song."

The serious-minded Shankly certainly developed an emotional attachment to the song. When Liverpool's charismatic manager appeared on *Desert Island Discs* in the spring of 1965, the Pacemakers' recording of 'You'll Never Walk Alone' was his final choice. Fittingly, it also closed his funeral service in 1981.

His granddaughter Karen Gill recollects how, in his dotage, he would "pull out his big gramophone and put the record on and play it, so we would hear it throughout the house". When the ornate Shankly Gates were unveiled on the Anfield Road 11 months after the great man's passing, the title of the Kopite anthem seemed an obvious choice to adorn them.

Tragically, the iconic phrase would assume even greater resonance as the Eighties progressed. In the dark days before the Taylor Report led to increased safety measures in stadiums across the country, 'You'll Never Walk Alone' soundtracked the two events that became a watershed in British football culture.

In 1985, the main stand of Bradford City's Valley Parade was engulfed in flames, killing 56 spectators and injuring at least 265 more. It was the final game of the season and had begun in celebratory fashion with the Bantams being presented with the Division Three championship trophy. 11,076 supporters, nearly double the season's average, were present to witness the scenes. Long before cameras were routinely found at every stadium in the Football League, the match against Lincoln City was being recorded by Yorkshire Television for the regional edition of ITV's Sunday afternoon football show *The Big Match*. When, shortly before half-time, a discarded cigarette slipped through the wooden floorboards and ignited a major build-up of litter in the cavity below, images of the resulting fire were broadcast on ITV's *World of Sport* and BBC's *Grandstand* to shocked viewers tuning in to hear the final scores. A disaster appeal fund was set up within 48 hours and would eventually raise over £3.5 million, one of the biggest contributors to which was a charity single spearheaded by Gerry Marsden.

Quickly recognising the pertinence of his biggest hit, Marsden assembled supergroup the Crowd to re-record 'You'll Never Walk Alone'. Thousands of tone-deaf football fans had already proven that the song's tender pathos was indestructible, and so it followed that a motley collection of musicians and showbiz personalities,including Bruce Forsyth, Keith Chegwin, Peter Cook, Dave Lee Travis,

Motörhead, Black Lace and Zak Starkey (son of Ringo) was able to propel the record from an initial chart placing of 52 to number one between 26 May and 9 June (overtaking Everton's 1985 FA Cup Final song 'Here We Go' on its way). Gerry and the Pacemakers made chart history in 1963 as the first act to reach number one with each of their first three singles, although 'Ferry Cross the Mersey' — the other song for which they're best known and indelibly linked with Liverpool — only peaked at number eight. The feat of a debut hat-trick had only very recently been matched by fellow Liverpudlians Frankie Goes to Hollywood (and subsequently by Jive Bunny and B*witched, amply demonstrating that there's really no accounting for the taste of the record-buying public of Great Britain). Marsden was able to reclaim a record of his own with the repeat success of 'You'll Never Walk Alone': the first person to top the charts with different versions of the same song.

Despite being convened in aid of Bradford City, it's probably fair to say that the Crowd is still just as readily associated with Liverpool thanks to the choice of song and the involvement of one of the city's favourite sons, besides Gerry; Paul McCartney was unable to attend the studio recording but he was undoubtedly the most famous person to contribute to the B-side 'Messages', a series of sympathetic words of solidarity in keeping with the A-side and the charitable cause.

So, Gerry and the Kop may have taken ownership of 'You'll Never Walk Alone' and given it a life beyond *Carousel*, but it definitely isn't theirs alone. In the lockdown days of April 2020, the baritone Michael Ball combined with the phenomenon of Captain Tom Moore and the NHS Voices of Care Choir to take the song to number one yet again, just in time for Captain Tom's 100th birthday, the track's timeless virtues thus making the corona-fundraising veteran the world's oldest ever chart-topper. Walk on indeed! And just a month earlier, continuing the cross-pollination of British and American culture that Marsden had helped to kick off six decades previously, Marcus Mumford, lead singer of South London folk-rockers Mumford & Sons, released a version originally recorded for the season one finale of the Apple TV+ soccer comedy *Ted Lasso*.

In an era of rampant globalisation, it should come as no great surprise that a popular song has spread far and wide, yet it's unusual how many different football clubs it has attached itself to. Besides the associations with Liverpool, Bradford and AFC Richmond, the 'Walk on, walk on' refrain also receives at least a semi-regular airing at Celtic Park (Scotland), Westfalenstadion (Borussia Dortmund, Germany), De Grolsch Veste (FC Twente, the Netherlands), De Kuip (Feyenoord, also the Netherlands), the Jan Breydel Stadium (Club Brugge, Belgium) and Ajinomoto (FC Tokyo, Japan). The biggest of those — Celtic and Dortmund — can actually be traced back to Liverpool, dating back to their encounters in the 1966 European Cup Winners' Cup semi-final and final, respectively. The Reds can't, however, claim any credit for its infiltration of Croatian ice hockey, other than setting an example of a well-timed musical interjection into a rapturous sporting environment.

It was a harmonious crowd atmosphere that inspired Queen to compose the equally symphonic 'We Will Rock You' and 'We Are the Champions'. In the middle of a successful 1977 tour, the operatic rock gods played Bingley Hall in Stafford. While not exactly rivalling the Sex Pistols gig at Manchester's Lesser Free Trade Hall for cultural import, its expressly non-punk moment came when, at the end of the show, rather than heading straight for the exits, the audience broke into an impromptu chorus of 'You'll Never Walk Alone'. Maybe there were some Liverpool fans in the crowd; the Reds had not been in nearby Wolverhampton or Stoke that day but they were riding a wave of jubilation from conquering Europe for the first time, beating Borussia Mönchengladbach 3-1 in the European Cup Final in midweek. Whatever the source of the recital, guitarist Brian May later told Radio 1: "We were just completely knocked out and taken aback — it was quite an emotional experience really." The band conspired to produce an anthemic chant of their own, yielding independent efforts that were then paired together as a double A-side: Freddie Mercury's bombastic 'We Are the Champions', now routinely played to accompany trophy presentations, and May's nursery rhyme-esque 'We Will Rock You' with its crowd-pleasing syncopation of stomps and handclaps.

Pink Floyd had earlier incorporated 'You'll Never Walk Alone' into the rock pantheon by sampling it on stoner classic 'Fearless', taken from 1971 album *Meddle*, which straddled the early Syd Barrett incarnation of the band and the prog-rock stylings of David Gilmour and Roger Waters. Superficially, Rodgers and Hammerstein's sampled mantra — a field recording from the Kop that is dropped deep in the mix near the start and comes to the fore like a Gregorian chant after five minutes — seems a natural fit for a song about rising to the challenge in the face of adversity. Mick McStarkey of *Far Out Magazine*, however, has identified the track as a "clever spoof", based on the fact that Waters, Gilmour and Nick Mason are all hardcore Arsenal fans. There had apparently been serious consideration given to calling album closer, the 23-minute opus 'Echoes', 'We Won the Double' in honour of the Gunners' historic league and cup triumphs in the summer preceding *Meddle*'s release. The 1971 FA Cup Final had been a 2-1 comeback victory against none other than Liverpool; McStarkey therefore interprets the inclusion of their opponent's anthem as an in-your-face irony and the line 'Fearlessly, the idiot faced the crowd, smiling' as a mocking reference to Shankly with the score stood at 0-1 ...

Aretha and Elvis adopted a far more reverent approach with gospel-tinged takes that backed songsmith Irving Berlin's opinion of 'You'll Never Walk Alone' as a modern hymn, like Psalm 23 ('The Lord is my shepherd, I shall not want ... ') set to music. The sheet music was a big seller across America and it quickly became a funeral staple. When the singer Mel Tormé told Richard Rodgers that the tune made him cry, the composer replied, "It's supposed to", explaining how he'd matched Oscar Hammerstein II's words to a march in 4/4 time that rises and falls like a sigh. Rodgers, incidentally, was upset at his song being appropriated for mass chanting at sports stadia and even consulted his lawyers to see if he could put a stop to this "travesty of [his] musical intentions" before reluctantly deciding against legal action when informed that there was no way to enforce a ban. The perfectionist composer liked his work to be performed just as he'd intended it; upon hearing Peggy Lee's jazzed-up version of his gentle waltz 'Lover', he is alleged to have scolded her, "Why pick on me when you could have f**ked up 'Silent Night'?"

Back to the Eighties, and maybe the late Rodgers (he died in 1979) would have approved of his song's healing qualities being applied to the second of British football's defining tragedies. From Broadway to Bradford via Munich and Manchester, the song has always stalked pain and grief but it reached its apogee with the 1989 Hillsborough tragedy that claimed the lives of 97 Liverpool supporters. In the aftermath, with tabloid newspapers falsely accusing a hooligan element for the fatal crush that occurred at Sheffield Wednesday's stadium, hosting the fateful FA Cup semi-final between Liverpool and Nottingham Forest, the notion of walking through a storm with your head held high had never rung truer to grieving Liverpudlians. Football is a tribal game but it also has an unrivalled power to unify and suddenly 'You'll Never Walk Alone' could be heard on both sides of Stanley Park, the natural soundtrack to city-wide vigils. It was written in the stars that Liverpool would prevail over Forest in the rearranged fixture at Old Trafford, setting up an all-Mersey final against Everton at Wembley, where Gerry Marsden would lead Reds and Blues alike through both the traditional cup final hymn 'Abide With Me' and his own abiding hit; if 'YNWA' wasn't already enshrined in Liverpool folklore then it certainly was from this moment on.

Of course, 'You'll Never Walk Alone' is not the only song to be heard from the Kop. There has even been published *The Anfield Songbook: We Have Dreams and Songs to Sing* (2017). Sadly not heard from the stands, barring the fact that it contains a warped staccato sample of 'YNWA', is 'Anfield Rap' — perhaps spectators simply feel too daunted to mimic the legendary rap stylings of John Barnes and pals.

If the mid-20th century was characterised by a shift from the recording studio to football stadia, with pop songs being adopted as club anthems, then the late-20th century witnessed a move in the opposite direction, with footballers trying their luck as pop stars. For all the derision thrown the way of the 1988 squad, exacerbated by Wimbledon's giant-killing in the FA Cup Final that 'Anfield Rap (Red Machine in Full Effect)' accompanied, hidden amongst the dubious hip-hop delivery there is actually some astute social commentary to be found. The forced rhyme of 'I come from Jamaica, my name is John Barn-es / When I do my thing, the crowd go bananas' doesn't possess the violent celestial imagery of dreams being tossed and blown, yet it could easily be read as a subversively defiant take on a notorious incident from earlier that year, when Barnes casually backheeled a banana thrown at him by a racist Everton fan. Born in Kingston, Jamaica, but bred nearer Kingston upon Thames, a humorous recognition of the England international's dual identity segues into a wry observation on regional disparities:

How's he doing the Jamaica rap?
He's from just south of the Watford Gap
He gives us stick about the north/south divide
'Cause they got the jobs
Yeah, but we got the side

The recognition of Liverpool's high unemployment rate and unfavourable position in Thatcher's post-industrial Britain is tackled with a disarming self-deprecation that preempted *Harry Enfield and Chums*' Scousers telling everyone to "Calm down, calm down!" and blunts parodies of the signature tune such as 'You'll Never Work Again' and the threatening-sounding 'You'll Never Walk Again', in which the affable Britpoppers Supergrass (from genteel Oxford) subvert the lyrical machismo of terrace chants with a mellower than mellow musical accompaniment. Such distortions might be insulting to the Liverpudlian character but should be taken as a backhanded compliment in opposition fans realising the anthem's power and trying to twist it to their own ends. Through challenging social climates, Liverpool FC has been the balm, providing a weather-beaten city with a sense of pride. It is implicit in 'You'll Never Walk Alone', but 'Anfield Rap' puts a specifically late-Eighties spin on these themes.

And if 'You'll Never Walk Alone' speaks of standing together, then 'Anfield Rap' also demonstrates an admirably inclusive spirit. With foreign imports on the verge of flooding into the British game, the native Scousers (John Aldridge and Steve McMahon) are tasked with inducting the lads 'from all over the place' into the Liverpool way and teaching them 'the song you've gotta learn', cue sample (which funnily enough must have received the blessing of Rodgers and Hammerstein's publishers or their estate to be licensed for the mechanical recording rights). Meshing Rodgers and Hammerstein with the Beatles ('Twist and Shout'), LL Cool J ('Rock the Bells'), Eric B. and Rakim ('I Know You Got Soul') and Run-DMC ('Here We Go'), the novelty record certainly embraced diversity and 'we'll just let our feet do the talking' stands as an early anti-racism message, even if references to the Irish contingent as 'Paddies' jar in 21st-century ears. South African-born Australian midfielder Craig Johnston is credited as a co-writer, alongside Paul Gainford, British rap pioneer Derek B and Ian Garfield Hoxley of Gaye Bykers on Acid, Pop Will Eat Itself, Pigface and Apollo 440. For all the ridicule heaped on the 'Anfield Rap', it represents the biggest hit in the careers of all the professional musicians involved and charted higher (number three) than any other Liverpool FC effort. The so-called 'Spice Boys' also felt compelled to record their own version in 1996, in conjunction with the brand new 'Pass and Move (It's the Liverpool Groove)', supported by the Back Room Boyz, a local collective that consisted of moonlighting Apollo 440 band members.

For all its merits, however, 'Anfield Rap' is never likely to be heard at a civil rights rally. When Wembley Stadium hosted An International Tribute for a Free South Africa in April 1990, marking the long-awaited release from prison of anti-apartheid campaigner Nelson Mandela, the guest of honour walked on stage to a standing ovation and a burst of 'You'll Never Walk Alone'. When Mandela asked what the amassed crowd of 74,000 were singing, wife Winnie reportedly replied, "I think it's a football song". Any suggestion that this moment inspired the title of his renowned autobiography is pure speculation.

Reviews

"There's not one club in Europe with an anthem like 'You'll Never Walk Alone'. There's not one club in the world so united with the fans. I sat there watching the Liverpool fans and they sent shivers down my spine. A mass of 40,000 people became one force behind their team."

– legendary Dutch purveyor of 'Total Football', Johan Cruyff

"When they start singing 'You'll Never Walk Alone', my eyes start to water. There have been times when I've actually been crying while I've been playing."

– the over-emotional Kevin Keegan, who represented Liverpool between 1971 and 1977

"As well as being a footballing song, it also filled a huge void for people who lost somebody at Hillsborough. It was emotive for many reasons, football was one of them, but not the most important one."

– Kenny Dalglish, Liverpool legend and player-manager at the time of the Hillsborough disaster

"We could hear our fans. Even in the dressing room we could pick out 'You'll Never Walk Alone'. I wouldn't say our supporters sounded defiant or full of belief. It was more the sound of solidarity. It lifted us."

– Steven Gerrard, on trailing AC Milan 3-0 in the 'Miracle of Istanbul' 2005 Champions League Final

"Some people say to me, it's like a prayer ... Every night on stage, I sing a prayer, so I must be going to heaven, surely."

– Gerry Marsden

2. Blue Moon

First released: 1934
Highest UK chart position: 1

For Shankly, Paisley and Klopp, read Lennon, McCartney and the Teardrop Explodes. For Busby, Ferguson and Guardiola, read Joy Division, New Order and the Smiths. Swap Anfield and Old Trafford for the Cavern and the Haçienda. Substitute Dalglish, Rush and Gerrard for the La's, Cilla and the Bunnymen; Best, Bell and Rooney for the Stone Roses, Happy Mondays and Take That.

Forget the Beatles versus the Stones or Blur versus Oasis. Although Arsène Wenger's Arsenal and José Mourinho's Chelsea mounted a temporary challenge to the dominance of the North West and reinforced the North-South divide, the real rivalry in the realms of both football and music foments at opposing ends of the M62. Apologies to Everton, who are unrepresented above save Rooney crossing boundaries, but the Mersey blues' rare periods of pre-eminence have generally coincided with the Mersey Reds, thus lessening the levels of inter-city acrimony stemming to and from Goodison Park. And in truth, Manchester City have only been part of the competition since Sheikh Mansour's billions propelled them to the top of the table.

Given the intensity of the regional rivalry, it is faintly ironic that Richard Rodgers follows the uncommon likes of Busby, Rooney and Paul Ince by making himself at home in both camps. Just as footballers are available to the highest bidder, Rodgers was a songwriter for hire, contracted to Hollywood studio MGM back in the 1930s when 'Blue Moon' first saw the light of day.

Rodgers and Lorenz Hart (forming a mean strike partnership before Hammerstein was transferred in for the ailing lyricist) were contracted to write songs for *Hollywood Party*, a star-studded movie revue featuring Laurel and Hardy. It was the kind of film that Gerry Marsden might have enjoyed, having only stumbled across 'You'll Never Walk Alone' because *Carousel* was on a double-bill with the complementary comedy duo. How transformed the audio landscape of British football might have been had the stars aligned slightly differently.

MGM Song No. 225, tentatively titled 'Prayer', failed to make the final cut of *Hollywood Party.* Hart subsequently wrote a new set of lyrics and re-titled the song 'It's Just That Kind of Play' for inclusion in the 1934 film *Manhattan Melodrama*, but it again went unused. The producers did, however, request a sultry number for a nightclub scene, so the tune was recycled into 'The Bad in Every Man' and, third time lucky, made it to the screen. After release, Jack Robbins, head of studio publishing, saw commercial potential, on the proviso that the tune be fitted with more romantic lyrics and a catchier title and so, finally, MGM Song No. 225 became 'Blue Moon'.

The story of its journey from Manhattan to Manchester is also full of false starts. Is the connection a simple one of colour? Well, partly, in that the sky-blue strip makes 'Blue Moon' far better suited to City than it ever could be to Manchester United or Liverpool. And team colours are important, hence City super-fan Adam 'Rage' White admitting that he's voted Conservative all his life purely on the basis of the party's 'true-blue' branding. But there's a little more to it than that, otherwise the Etihad Stadium could trill to 'Blue Velvet', 'Blue Jay Way' or 'Blue Monday'.

Chances are, with the advent of tannoy systems and stadium DJs in the early Sixties, 'Blue Moon' would have been aired at Maine Road at some point before the apocryphal tales of how it actually caught on in the late-Eighties/early-Nineties. The song has been performed by a litany of big names, including Elvis and Sinatra (again), Ella Fitzgerald, Billie Holiday, Bob Dylan and even (in demo form) the Beatles, though it was doo-wop group the Marcels who rocketed it to the top of the charts in 1961. Any chance of its early adoption was stymied by City finishing a disappointing 13th that season, the mundanity of it making their fans disinclined to sing. It could have been resurrected by an innovative DJ when they won the league seven years later, but it wasn't to be. At least, not yet.

Anyway, the City of old was not a club predicated on success. Quite the opposite, in fact — club historian Gary James recalls 'Blue Moon' first being sung after a 3-1 defeat at Anfield on the opening day of the 1989-90 season. With the away end detained after the final whistle, and perhaps wishing to dislodge the home fans' anthem from their inner ears, some of the lads launched into the 'other' Rodgers composition, the rest joined in, and then kept it going when they next congregated for a game at home to Southampton.

Away fans certainly tend to be the most vociferous and an alternative take on the song's City origins takes us back to the 1986-87 season, when they failed to win a single game on the road and were subsequently relegated. 'Blue Moon' was a product of gallows humour: with the winless streak away from home stretching back to January 1986, the phrase 'once in a blue moon', referring to the rare astronomical event in the lunar cycle that a full moon appears twice in a calendar month, was regularly applied to their chances of winning, including in a TV interview by manager Howard Kendall. It took two seasons to regain their top-flight status and then until 1 April 1990 to finally break a run of 41 gloomy awaydays against top-tier opposition. So when they amazingly did so, at title-chasing

Villa, 'Blue Moon' rang out at the Witton End from fans driven close to their wits' end. They would then go unbeaten in their remaining four away games, winning another two, so 'Blue Moon' morphed quickly from black comedy to lucky charm.

Fully accustomed to playing second fiddle to the Reds at that point in time, the Citizens should nevertheless be miffed at being runners-up to Crewe Alexandra, for it was the Railwaymen who supposedly first adopted 'Blue Moon'. There is some debate over how much they beat City by, with some sources dating it very specifically to an away game at Stockport County on 22 April 1988 in memoriam to the 1950s, while others contest that it was actually sung back then, before even the Marcels but at the same time as Elvis Presley.

And the reasons for singing? Much the same as City's. In fact, Crewe's era of underachievement far surpasses their north-west neighbours. In 1951, they suffered their heaviest ever defeat (an 11-1 tonking at the hands of Lincoln City) and then spent a good chunk of the decade without an away win, 56 games in total, while rooted to the foot of the Football League. The hardy souls who endured this picked up on Rodgers and Hart's melancholic ballad as a testament to both Alex's cobalt away kit and the infrequency with which they won.

It would take a bit of 'Sunchyme' to dispel the blues around Gresty Road, for the Nineties happy-house ditty by Dario G is not the work of a swarthy Sicilian knob-twiddler, but a trio of Crewevians paying homage to their team's long-serving manager, Dario Gradi. Furthering their football pedigree, follow-up 'Carnaval de Paris' was an unofficial anthem to the France '98 World Cup, incorporating strains of a popular terrace chant based on folk ballad 'Oh My Darling, Clementine'.

So, Man City fans were not entirely alone in serenading the titular blue moon, but neither they nor the Crewe supporters had much of a dream in their hearts. Until, that is, September 2008, when the Abu Dhabi royal family expanded its sports portfolio and suddenly, as per the song's lyrics, 'the moon had turned to gold'.

City's new owners didn't just invest in players. Endemol, the media behemoth behind *Big Brother*, *Deal or No Deal* and *Golden Balls* to name just a few, were commissioned to produce a documentary covering the first full season of the Sheikh's reign. The cameras caught the high-profile signings of Carlos Tevez and Emmanuel Adebayor, the appointment of Roberto Mancini, and a climb from mid-table mediocrity to narrowly missing out on Champions League football. For a title, they turned to the fan anthem, symbolising a connection to the club's heritage, but added a verb indicating its upward trajectory: *Blue Moon Rising*. Initially slated for broadcast on TV, the club's growing ambitions were matched with a limited cinematic release, the red carpet replaced by a blue one, which brought 'Blue Moon' full circle from *Hollywood Party*.

The song naturally features prominently but the producers missed a trick by not inviting one of Manchester's musical alumni to re-record it. Noel Gallagher — heavily featured as a Man City devotee — would later nick the title, but his own 'Blue Moon Rising' is not obviously an ode to his team's meteoric ascent. Given Noel's fondness for gibberish lyrics, it would probably be wrong to read any more into the name than that he liked the sound of it, although there are faint echoes of Hart's imagery and City's fortunes in lines like 'Will I meet you down on the corner / Where our hopes and dreams were sold?'. The man himself has been uncharacteristically reticent on its City connections, though the average fan can probably relate to his assertion regarding 'Champagne Supernova' and music in general, that "it means different things when I'm in different moods".

Matchday organisers had already used various recordings of 'Blue Moon' as walk-out music, with players emerging from the tunnel to both Supra's punk version (also used by City fan Ricky Hatton for his ring-walk) and Doves' choral interpretation. Then, for the start of the 2011-12 season — the one in which Sergio Agüero's last-gasp winner against Queens Park Rangers would snatch the Premier League crown from Manchester United, marking a distinct power shift between the world's biggest club™ and their noisy neighbours — Oasis offshoot Beady Eye covered the club anthem for the promotional launch of the new home kit, featuring frontman Liam kissing the badge. In typically self-effacing fashion, he told the *NME*, "'Blue Moon' is a top tune and has been City's song for as long as I can remember. It's been covered by loads of people but the only good one until now was the one Elvis did." He also joked that his football and musical destinies were diametrically opposed: "When Oasis were doing well, City were doing shit. But now we've split, City are doing good."

What price an Oasis reunion heralding a swing from 'Blue Moon' back to 'Glory, Glory Man United'?

Reviews

"There's a melancholy to it. That's been borne out of 30 or 40 years living in United's shadow. Being relegated and relegated again. We don't have the 'Glory, Glory Man United' type stuff. United fans live in London. The Mancunian soundtrack, bar 'Blue Moon', is steeped in the city. People will never understand it until they live in Manchester."

– Noel Gallagher discussing the songs that accompanied Manchester City's treble celebrations, also including his own 'Don't Look Back in Anger', Inspiral Carpets' 'This Is How It Feels' and Joy Division's 'Love Will Tear Us Apart'

"City since I can remember... Started going to the Etihad with my mum every weekend, singing 'Blue Moon' from the stands like every other fan ... The future is blue."

– Stockport-born teenager Phil Foden explaining his connection to the club on the day he signed a long-term contract in 2018

"When I first went on Sky as the main support they said I needed some music for my ring walk. There was only one song really. I think I'm probably the only man who has got United fans singing 'Blue Moon'."

– multi-time world champion boxer Ricky Hatton, writing in *The Times* on the day of Manchester City's 2023 Champions League triumph

"Maine Road remains a tremendously special part of the city to all Manchester City fans. You can feel the emotion whenever you drive to that part of the city and I think this is a wonderful idea."

– City legend Mike Summerbee (whose 357 appearances predate the song's terrace adoption, which coincided more closely with his son Nicky's career) on the laying of a blue tarmac pathway in Moss Side, aptly named Blue Moon Way, to commemorate Manchester City's first league title in 44 years

3. I'm Forever Blowing Bubbles

First released: 1918
Highest UK chart position: 31

Are any football anthems actually celebratory?! West Ham United's song of choice begins with an air of optimism and gaiety but those metaphorical bubbles — symbolic of rising hopes and expectations — are quickly popped. The beauty of the song is that its subject is not dejected by failure and will keep on blowing *forever*, like an extended version of the widespread '____ till I die' chant that encapsulates the staunch loyalty of football fans. In accordance with this willingness to absorb heartbreak and go again, Hammers fans sing the chorus of 'Bubbles' on loop, even though there are lesser-known verses that point towards a possible happy ending — 'Happiness new seemed so near me / Happiness come forth and heal me'.

In many ways, the lyrical narratives of this and 'Blue Moon' mirror the ebb and flow of a football match. 'Without a dream in my heart' takes on 'They fly so high' (West Ham take the lead) ... 'You knew just what I was there for' hits back at 'Like my dreams they fade and die' (City find a second wind and exploit West Ham's soft underbelly to equalise) … 'The moon had turned to gold' overcomes 'Fortune's always hiding' — City emerge victorious.

Win, lose or draw, 'Bubbles' is heard around the London Stadium, just as it was at the Boleyn before it, suggesting that all those descending suds have somehow seeped into the fabric of the club. Perhaps only 'You'll Never Walk Alone' can rival it for being representative of a club's culture, since the renowned 'West Ham Way' is predicated on effervescence: like the bubbles, their traditional playing style is pleasing on the eye, but ultimately ineffectual. Even the World Cup-winning class of '66 could only finish 12th, and West Ham's highest league placing during the Hurst-Moore-Peters golden period was a modest eighth, albeit with an FA Cup and European Cup Winners' Cup to keep the dreamers dreaming of greater glory.

The club even took the first line of the first verse literally — 'I'm dreaming dreams, I'm scheming schemes, I'm building castles high' — by adorning the 2001 redevelopment of the Boleyn Ground's West Stand with faux turrets, although this was officially in tribute to Green Street House, more commonly known as Boleyn Castle, from which the ground, although more commonly known as Upton Park, took its name. Legend has it that this is where Henry VIII courted Anne Boleyn, before Green Street became more commonly associated with rampaging hooligans than adulterous royals.

Despite this architectural crossover, 'I'm Forever Blowing Bubbles' didn't originally have any links to the East End. It is instead another example of the cultural crossover that has seen fiercely nationalistic football fans appropriate songs from a country that largely ignores our national sport and instead plays football with its hands.

The tune was another hit from the Tin Pan Alley stable of songwriters and publishers that included Rodgers, Hammerstein, Hart and other luminaries such as Irving Berlin, George Gershwin and Frank Loesser. The music was composed by New England songwriter John Kellette and it debuted in Broadway musical revue *The Passing Show of 1918*, with lyrics credited to Jaan Kenbrovin, which transpired to be a composite pseudonym of James Kendis (hailing from Minnesota), James Brockman (born Jacob Brachman, a New York-Russian immigrant) and Nat Vincent (from Missouri). There's a loose Hollywood connection in *The Passing Show of 1918* featuring a young Fred Astaire, though he wasn't involved in the number. A Ben Selvin's Novelty Orchestra recording in 1919 was one of that year's 78rpm phonograph record bestsellers stateside. The same year also witnessed its sporting debut when esteemed sports columnist and short-story scribe Ring Lardner wrote a parody, 'I'm Forever Blowing Ballgames', about the Black Sox Scandal, in which members of the Chicago White Sox were accused of throwing baseball's World Series to the Cincinnati Reds. It also features extensively in James Cagney's 1931 gangster movie *The Public Enemy.*

'Bubbles' drifted across the Atlantic and became a crowd-pleaser in British music halls, most famously performed by actress-singer Dorothy Ward, who had a lucrative livelihood playing the principal boy in pantomimes and was allegedly lusted after by Winston Churchill, despite her hard-drinking husband Shaun Glenville playing the pantomime dame opposite. Ward and Glenville (who was also an amateur songwriter) toured the country, with no particular affiliation to the East End, which despite being a bastion of music hall traditions still does not provide a clear thoroughfare for 'Bubbles' to reach the Boleyn.

Contrary to popular belief, 'Bubbles' was not heard at the famous 1923 White Horse Final, when West Ham met Bolton Wanderers at the first Wembley showpiece. According to club historian John Helliar, a souvenir leaflet of the occasion instead contains lyrics to be sung to the refrain of 'Till We Meet Again', a not dissimilar waltz also written in the last year of the Great War and later popularised by both Doris Day and Huddersfield Town, who rechristened it 'Smile Awhile'. The first spontaneous outbreak of 'Bubbles' at Wembley came in the 1940 League War Cup Final, a tournament established to fill the wartime void in the football calendar in which West Ham beat Blackburn Rovers 1-0. Though the Blitz had yet to take hold, the never-say-die, underdog spirit of 'I'm Forever Blowing Bubbles' spoke to embattled EastEnders, and singalongs in pubs and bunkers helped keep morale high. The 'Forces' Sweetheart' Vera Lynn, born in East Ham, would later release one of the best-known versions of the song.

The bond between song and club, however, had already been forged in the most tenuous manner imaginable. At a time when music hall was the height of entertainment, schoolboy soccer was also extremely popular and attendances on the touchlines of park pitches could exceed 1,000. One of the most successful academies was Park School, situated on Ham Park Road, bordering West Ham Park. Headmaster Cornelius Beal was an avid football fan and enthusiastic lyricist. Not content with watching his boys trample the opposition, he also supposedly had a habit of regaling star players with song: a proto-terrace wordsmith. One such star player was Billy J. 'Bubbles' Murray, so-called because of a passing resemblance to the boy in the 1886 painting by Sir John Everett Millais, formally titled *A Child's World* but more commonly known as 'Bubbles'. Park School didn't specialise in art history as well as P.E.; the painting had been made famous for its use advertising Pears Soap, so Murray's nickname was the equivalent of children from the late-Sixties to the early-Noughties being dubbed the Milkybar Kid by dint of having fair hair and glasses. Music hall and boys' football converged, with 'I'm Forever Blowing Bubbles' being the obvious choice of song with which Beal could serenade Murray, in the days before such activities could have raised some serious safeguarding concerns.

Murray was part of the West Ham Boys team of 1920-21 that played Liverpool Boys at Upton Park in the English Shield Championship Final, in front of a record 30,000 crowd which included the Duke of York, the future King George VI. Several of Murray's teammates were also Park School classmates, so it is entirely likely that a Beal rendition was the first time 'I'm Forever Blowing Bubbles' was heard at the Boleyn. Appropriately enough, Liverpool Boys staged a comeback to win 3-2. This was also as high as Murray's fledgling football career would fly; the promising schoolboy would never make it to the professional ranks, yet his impact on the club remains significantly greater than many of those who did.

Besides being headmaster and self-appointed cheerleader, Beal was also friends with Charlie Paynter, who was promoted from long-serving coach to manager of West Ham in 1932. Before pre-match DJs and pop tunes, it was customary for house bands to entertain the masses ahead of kick-off and it was purportedly at Paynter's request that 'I'm Forever Blowing Bubbles' was added to the repertoire. A former employee of the Beckton Gas Works recalled in the company's pensioners' bulletin in 1983 that the company band "were engaged by the West Ham United Football Club to play for 20 minutes before the kick-off and ten minutes at the interval. We played 'Bubbles' and it very quickly became a favourite with the crowd. If we did not play 'Bubbles' the crowd would sing it — so we always played it just before the kick-off."

The airiness of 'Bubbles' contrasts with the club's industrial origins as Thames Ironworks FC, which is commemorated in the Hammers nickname and the enduring 'Come on you Irons' chant. The hot-blooded rivalry with Millwall, founded by tinsmiths on the Isle of Dogs, derives from their early incarnations competing for shipbuilding contracts as well as sporting pride, hence the local skirmish being known as the Dockers Derby despite the clubs being far removed from these origins. The scurrilous rumour that Millwall sang 'Bubbles' first is therefore a source of even greater bitterness than 'You'll Never Walk Alone' making its debut at Old Trafford. There is, nevertheless, documentary evidence that 'Bubbles' was on the marching band playlist at the Den as early as 1922.

There is also conjecture that Swansea Town (now City) brought 'Bubbles' to the attention of West Ham fans during a marathon FA Cup tie in 1921. Contemporary news articles confirm that the Welsh were early proponents of terrace singing and that 'Bubbles' was a staple:

> "Then came the ever popular 'Bubbles', and the crowd simply yelled. The spectators on the main bank took their cue from the Mumbles end, and there was one tremendous sway, together with the singing, on the part of about 25,000 spectators. Some embraced one another, and suddenly thousands of white handkerchiefs were waved high above the heads of the owners."
>
> (*The Sporting News*, 8 January 1921, reporting on Swansea vs Bury)

After a goalless draw at the Vetch Field, the teams drew 1-1 at the Boleyn before a further replay at the neutral territory of Bristol City's Ashton Gate saw Swansea eventually progress by a solitary goal. Some form of musical osmosis is entirely conceivable across several meetings in such close proximity. However, given the evident popularity of the song in the early Twenties, the most likely explanation is that it was adopted simultaneously, in much the same way as a current hit might receive exposure in multiple sporting arenas, but can only be laid claim to once time and tradition has tied it to a particular institution.

Unusually in the parochial world of football, 'Bubbles' has even been heard at opposition grounds in honour of West Ham United. On the final day of the 1994-95 season, Blackburn Rovers needed to beat Liverpool to secure the Premier League title. Failing to do so, they became reliant on West Ham denying Manchester United three points. Hammers goalkeeper Luděk Mikloško had the game of his life to keep the score at 1-1, and Shearer, Sutton, Sherwood et al. could celebrate becoming league champions. 'Bubbles' was heard emanating from the Blackburn dressing room, orchestrated by defender Tony Gale, who had spent a decade at West Ham before joining Blackburn at the start of that season.

A similar scenario played out on the final day of the 2005-06 season, when Tottenham Hotspur needed to beat West Ham to savour their first taste of Champions League football. 'Lasagne-gate' — in which a large number of the squad were struck down with suspected food poisoning — condemned Spurs to defeat, thereby gifting the final Champions League position to Arsenal, who beat Wigan Athletic 4-2 in the final match at Highbury. Unable to resort to their habitual 'One-nil to the Ar-se-nal', Gunners supporters instead taunted mutual rivals Tottenham by loudly parading West Ham's club anthem.

They are, thus far, the only two times that 'Bubbles' has accompanied top-flight triumph or Champions League qualification, although it had enjoyed previous outings at Wembley in 1975 and 1980. On the first occasion, to mark an FA Cup Final against Fulham, it was recorded and released by the West Ham United Cup Squad and peaked at number 31 in the charts. It must have been a disorientating experience for Bobby Moore to hear his ex-teammates on record before stepping out for his last match at Wembley in the black and white of Fulham, having parted company with West Ham the season before. Perhaps even more discombobulating is the punk thrash of 'Bobby Moore Was Innocent', in which Norwich band Serious Drinking (favourites of John Peel in the early-Eighties) recount the classy defender's arrest for an alleged jewellery theft in Bogotá, Colombia on the eve of the 1970 World Cup.

Mining a similar element, the Cockney Rejects were responsible for the 1980 recording to mark a cup final appearance against Arsenal. EMI wanted to cash in and it was a toss-up between the Rejects and Iron Maiden, both of whom released their debut album in early-'80 and both of whom were native Irons (Steve Harris, Maiden founder and bassist, was scouted in his teens by the legendary Wally St Pier, who was appointed club chief scout by Paynter and was also responsible for recruiting a young John Lyall, Bobby Moore and Trevor Brooking among many others). After seeing off Iron Maiden (who revived club links in 2019 with the Die With Your Boots On collaborative clothing range), the 'Oi!' pioneers shamefully charted four places lower than their 1975 predecessors, but their spikier version, which smacks of bubbles popping in everyone's faces, has stood the test of time far better. Speaking in 2021, vocalist Jeff

Geggus, aka Stinky Turner, ruminated on football firms and the unwelcome far-right ('bullies… we were deadly opposed to these people') targeting the band:

> "Football was very entwined with music. People might say it was a bad thing because it brought violence at gigs, but maybe we wouldn't have stood out if we weren't connected with the football. It's got us where we are now, so a few regrets but it is what it is."

The ageing rockers were invited to perform at the Boleyn on the balmy evening in 2016 that West Ham bade farewell to their old ground, and they also issued the mellower commemorative track 'Goodbye Upton Park' (sample lyrics: 'Wherever you may roam / It will always be our home / Sing goodbye Upton Park').

Though the transition to the former Olympic Stadium site in Stratford has been far from smooth, true to their signature song the Hammers faithful have never stopped blowing bubbles. West Ham's change of abode means 'Bubbles' can also lay claim to appearing on perhaps the biggest sporting and entertainment stage of all; in a nod to its local environs and the stadium's legacy tenants, the London 2012 Olympic Opening Ceremony, directed by acclaimed filmmaker Danny Boyle, featured a burst of the famous chorus complemented by the visual spectacle of 30 giant bubble makers. In a separate part of the ceremony, multiple Mary Poppins descended from the night sky, minus Dick Van Dyke's one-man band and chimney sweep, Bert. Though Van Dyke's Mockney accent has been much ridiculed, some innovators in claret and blue upped the ante on the chirpy-chappy Cockney persona by setting a fast-paced run-through of Kenbrovin's lyrics to a Sherman brothers' composition from *Mary Poppins*' celluloid sibling, thus creating an early progenitor to the mash-up with the one-time fan favourite 'Chitty Chitty Bubbles'!

As if any further evidence were required of club embracing song, West Ham United FC got themselves in the *Guinness Book of World Records* for most people simultaneously blowing bubbles (23,680 before a Premier League home fixture against Middlesbrough on

16 May 1999). That record is surely ripe for breaking given that the London Stadium has nearly double the capacity of the Boleyn, and a new world record might have provided meagre consolation had the wait for a trophy gone on any longer. As it was, 43 years of dreams fading and dying ended with a dramatic UEFA Europa Conference League win in June 2023, sending W.H.A.M. Utd's version of alternative (and more narcissistic) terrace singalong 'West Ham Are Massive' into the upper echelons of the iTunes chart. Joining it on the celebration playlist was 'Bowen's on Fire', a risqué reworking of Nineties banger 'Freed from Desire' by Gala (previously reworked by Wigan fans in honour of winger Will Grigg), referencing the winning goalscorer's relationship with *Love Island* contestant Dani Dyer, who had just borne them twin girls, thereby verifying the chorus's twin claims about striker Jarrod: as paraphrased by doting new grandfather and professional *EastEnder* Danny Dyer, "Bowen's on fire ... and he's ... cuddling me daughter or something"!

One month after flouting their original anthem's premise by actually winning something, and as if to reassert the preferred East End underdog status in the face of having a European trophy and the second-highest average attendance in the Premier League, the club reiterated its fondness of 'Bubbles' by unveiling the new Anthem kit, with suds faintly imprinted onto the home shirts for the 2023-24 season: "The fabric of our club" was how the sales pitch put it.

Reviews

"We were just supporting our team. I mean, if someone had said to me a year before that West Ham were going to be in the Cup Final and that we'd be doing a punk version of 'Bubbles' on *Top of the Pops*, I would've never have believed them. So of course we were going to be lairy."

– Jeff Geggus (then 16 years old) on the Cockney Rejects being banned from the BBC in 1980

"The next time you hear the rousing terrace voices singing 'I'm Forever Blowing Bubbles' at the London Stadium, think of its bizarre genesis and William 'Bubbles' Murray, the local lad who never even made it to the first team on the pitch, but a West Ham legend that has lasted for over 100 years. And probably will last at least another 100."

– 'The One and Only' Chesney Hawkes, who performed in the Prague fan park on the day that his beloved West Ham won the 2023 Europa Conference League

"If we want to take back our freedom, we have to be smart, respectful and have to stay home. This is the only way we will be able to hug each other again just like before and sing your song. I'm forever blowing bubbles ..."

– maverick Italian Paolo Di Canio issued this public service announcement via YouTube during the coronavirus lockdown, April 2020; he proceeded to sing 'Bubbles' while doing keepy-uppies in a retro West Ham shirt

"Undoubtedly, 'I'm Forever Blowing Bubbles' holds a special place in the pantheon of football anthems. Its timeless appeal, evocative lyrics, and deep-rooted associations make it a powerful symbol of devotion and unwavering support, earning its place among the greatest football songs of all time."

– oldtimemusic.com

"Despite the name of my fanzine, I have always had mixed feelings about our anthem. On paper, it's such a depressingly glass-half-empty song and there's always someone who pops up every now and again to start a discussion about whether or not we need to change it to something that'll inspire the players more. But whenever you ask anyone who doesn't support West Ham to name things about the club, this anthem will always be one of the first things they'll say. And on a big night under the lights, there's nothing more goosebump-inducing than hearing 60,000+ fans singing 'I'm Forever Blowing Bubbles'."

– David Blackmore, editor of *Blowing Bubbles*

4. When the Saints Go Marching In

First released: unknown
Highest UK chart position: N/A

How can any association football team lay claim to an African-American spiritual song that is reckoned to have begun in the Bahamas and was popularised by the jazz bands of New Orleans?

Like the competing claims on the song's music publishing, many clubs do claim it as their own. Sometimes miscredited to Methodist music teacher Katherine E. Purvis (lyrics) and hymnal composer, choir leader and Sunday school preacher James M. Black (music) on the basis of the uncannily similar 'When the Saints Are Marching In' (1896), several others have tried to copyright their own arrangements, including southern gospel songwriter Luther G. Presley (no relation to Elvis, who sure enough recorded his own version in 1956). Just as Louis Armstrong, Judy Garland and Woody Guthrie have all put their own spin on the traditional chaunt, so have fans of Fulham ('Oh, when the Whites...'), Aberdeen ('Oh, when the Reds...') and Oldham ('Oh, when the Blues...') — spot the theme?

Full marks to Inverness Caledonian Thistle for being more lyrically imaginative by setting a tourist board promotion to the same melody: 'Oh Inverness is wonderful' punctuated by 'We've got a bridge and a castle'. The minor adjustment of 'marching' to 'steaming', employed by numerous tribes, has the fairly major impact of denoting hooliganism rather than holiness, as evidenced by *The Times of India* reporting on Bengaluru FC's usage giving the Indian Super League an "ultra" flavour. And Liverpool supposedly began singing it around the same time as they adopted 'You'll Never Walk Alone', in honour of illustrious forward and broadcaster-to-be Ian St John, vacillating between 'Saint' and 'Reds'. Similarly, St Johnstone, St Mirren and St Patrick's all have perfectly valid claims on the original arrangement. Nevertheless, we're crediting it to Southampton on the grounds of their spiritual connection.

The south coast club is sanctified by its nickname, borne of its origins as a church football team. Southampton have been otherwise known as '(the) Saints' since the club's inception in 1885 as St Mary's Church of England Young Men's Association FC. Quite a mouthful for chanting that; Saints certainly trips off the tongue easier, yet the song didn't migrate from the American South to the UK port city until the jazz explosion of the 1950s, when Louis 'Satchmo' Armstrong first visited these shores. In their early days playing on Southampton Common, it wasn't so much the saints marching in as ramblers, who would disrupt St Mary's matches by exercising their right to roam across the playing surface.

Prior to adopting 'When the Saints Go Marching In' as their theme tune, the Saints Supporters Association picked out a song linked by place rather than name. Lyricist Douglas Furber (most famous for 'The Lambeth Walk') met Australian composer A. Emmett Adams in Southampton during the First World War and, inspired by their surroundings, they wrote 'The Bells of St Mary's'. The song was a hit in the US, but overlooked in the UK, at least until it was revived by Bing Crosby in a 1945 film of the same name. In October 1950, local musician Monty Warlock was commissioned by the supporters association to pen some new lyrics:

The bells of St Mary's
A message are bringing
It's play up and win now
As cheers round you roll
So up for Saints and win boys
For victory we're singing
You've got 'em beat
We're on our feet
It's goal! Goal! Goal!

Adams' melody is rather sappy, so credit to Warlock for investing it with some oomph. His lyrics are also considerably more affirmative than those in 'When the Saints Go Marching In'. You thought the gospel hymn was upbeat? Even overlooking the spiritual's grim association with plantation songs and historical bondage, the standard lyrics are positively apocalyptic, derived from the Book of Revelation, albeit omitting some of the more horrific imagery of the Last Judgment. Football grounds only tend to hear the first verse, repeated ad nauseam. 'Oh, when the drums begin to bang' might also work on the terraces but supporters are best spared 'when the stars fall from the sky', 'when the moon turns red with blood' and 'when the horsemen begin to ride'. The saints marching in is not the depiction of a victory parade but a metaphor for the end of days, better suited to relegation than a morale-boosting advance.

Still, in the venerable tradition of dreams fading and the vast majority of football teams ending each season empty-handed, an apocalyptic ditty is not as incongruous as one might think. And the beauty of 'Saints' is its adaptability. Changing fortunes can be reflected by the tempo: just as the funeral rituals of New Orleans would see the jazz accompaniment rise from an elegiac pace to a more festive one as mourners moved from ceremony to wake, stadium chants can quickly go from a mournful 70 bpm to an excitable 140 bpm, representing either elation or defiance. Then there's the call and response version ('Oh when the saints' — 'Oh when the saints' — 'Go marching in' — 'Go marching in') which corresponds to the spirit of camaraderie in 'You'll Never Walk Alone'.

For a song about death rather than glory, it is perhaps fitting that none of the estimated thousand versions committed to vinyl, tape or cloud has ever featured in the UK singles chart, though had Bobby Stokes done a recording in 1976 then things might be different. Instead, Brummie comedian Jasper Carrott produced the only musical memorial of Southampton's crowning achievement by telling the story of 'Cup Final 76' in the style of a medieval folk ballad (featured on the 1976 live album *Carrott in Notts* alongside 'Top of the Pops', 'Football News' and 'I'm a Goalie You Know'). That year's cup final effort from the vanquished Manchester United was written by Tony Hiller, who had just won the Eurovision Song Contest with Brotherhood of Man and 'Save Your Kisses for Me'. Evidently he'd saved his best for Europe and not the unimaginatively titled 'Manchester United', which also recycled lyrics from his first Brotherhood of Man hit, 'United We Stand'. The B-side was the appropriately titled 'Old Trafford Blues', self-penned by United captain Martin Buchan and mocking his teammates' abilities. For example, of right-back Alex Forsyth, he sang, 'He's the one they call the ballboy's friend / His crosses to the far post land up in the Stretford End'!

Southampton again opted against recording an official song when they reached the 2003 FA Cup Final, so an enthusiastic batch of amateurs marched into the breach. Of the six known songs competing for the attention of Saints devotees, one was of course a souped-up version of their anthem. 'Oh When the Saints' by Saints Supporters — and produced by Barry Upton, a member of the Eighties incarnation of Brotherhood of Man and co-creator of the Camembert of Nineties/Noughties pop, Steps — failed to chart on either release; it had previously been issued in 2001 to commemorate the move to St Mary's Stadium and featured crowd recordings from the Dell. The B-side, 'Southampton, Southampton', featured the MC skills of Matthew Le Tissier, who frequently lit up the Dell but not so much St Mary's (he announced his retirement part-way through the first season there), nor the recording studio.

Scottish firebrand Gordon Strachan isn't noted for his musical talent either, but as then-Southampton manager he charitably lent his gravelly tones to Hook-with-Warsash School's 'We are the Saints, We're Strachan's Clan'. Written by music teacher Mr Baxter, with the Southampton manager laying down vocals alongside 400-plus schoolchildren, it's a bit St Winifred's School Choir meets the Firm, but can't be knocked since all proceeds went to Christian Aid.

The other 2003 releases were: 'We are Southampton Football Club (And We're Gonna Win the FA Cup)' by Mike Shannon (not to be confused with Mick Channon, having enjoyed some success on the local music scene in the Eighties rather than as a striker in the Seventies); 'Just Like 76' by compere and singer Martin Murphy, who boasts of playing the O2, St Mary's Stadium and Thorpe Park in support of the likes of Robbie Williams, Michael Bublé, McBusted, Peter Andre and Bradley Walsh; 'All Southampton' by Lloyd Two, consisting of the Payne brothers Russell, a financial advisor, and Adrian, an expert in merger control and competition authorities. Top of the pops, though, was 'Southampton Boys' by Red 'N' White Machines, which made it to number 16 in the national charts, backed by local radio station Power FM and the Artful Dodger's Mark Hill and MC Alistair.

If the unsuccessful assault on the charts in 2003 depicts Saints fans as a game bunch with musical ambitions beyond their talent, then the Red Stripez do nothing to dispel that notion. In 2015, the duo of James Knights and Mark Lawrence released 'Southampton in Europa' to celebrate the club's qualification for UEFA's secondary competition. Sadly, the Saints lost to FC Midtjylland of Denmark in the play-off round. Not to be discouraged, both came back the following year when automatic qualification through a sixth-place league position meant Southampton gracing the Europa League proper for the first time and a re-release for 'Southampton in Europa' in advance of their first match against Sparta Prague. Though Southampton won 3-0 on the night, they failed to progress past the group stage, and Sparta were eventual group winners.

For a musical analogy, the Red Stripez wouldn't even muster a shot on target against the Fall's 'Theme from Sparta FC'.

Regrettably, Craig David has not yet felt moved to rap about yo-yoing between divisions or past adventures in the Texaco Cup.

Reviews

"The sacrilegious desecration of Spirituals, the only real American music, as it is swung in gin shops, dance halls, over the radio and on records in various nondescript amusement places, is a disgrace to the whole race."

– Rev. George W. Harvey, responding to Louis Armstrong's version in 1939

"There is always one lighter question and on this occasion it was an invitation to name a favourite hymn and to sing the first two lines. Luckily it was the weekend that my football team, Southampton, nicknamed the Saints, were appearing in the FA Cup semi-final so I was able to make a reasonable fist of singing the club's anthem 'When the Saints Go Marching In'. The audience even joined in!"

– former British Prime Minister Rishi Sunak on his Radio 4 *Any Questions* panel discussion debut (at rishisunak.com, 11/05/18)

"Couldn't sleep until late because of the buzz of last night. Then wake up, wide awake at 4am with OH WHEN THE SAINTS…GO MARCHING IN. OH WHEN THE SAINTS GO MARCHING IN!! running through my mind #SaintsFC #CarabaoCup"

– cult hero Francis Benali posts to X (formerly Twitter) on 11 January 2023, the morning after Southampton triumphed 2-0 over Manchester City in the quarter-final of the League Cup

"The tightrope that I'm walking just sways and ties / The devil as he's talking with those angel's eyes / And I just want to be there when the lightning strikes / And the saints go marching in"

– Coldplay's 'Us Against the World' (2011) co-written by drummer and Southampton fan Will Champion, who has a season ticket with his dad and backed the Save Our Saints campaign in 2009; legend has it that backstage at the V Festival in 2000, Chris Martin pledged to buy Southampton FC for his friend and bandmate if they ever became mega-rich rock stars

5. On the Ball, City

First released: c.1890s
Highest UK chart position: N/A

The first entry to begin life as a football song, 'On the Ball, City' is generally regarded as the oldest one still in use and actually predates the club with which it is affiliated, Norwich City FC.

It is believed to have been written towards the end of the 19th century by Norfolk businessman Albert T. Smith (no known relation to Delia, who infamously attempted to rouse the masses many generations later) and used by a variety of local clubs including Norwich Teachers, Swifans and Caley's FC. Norwich City FC was not founded until 1902, and Smith became a club director in 1905, which is presumably when the song became theirs. He is reported to have sung it at a celebration event marking the club's entry into the professional ranks that same year.

Other contenders for earliest club-affiliated football songs include Wolverhampton Wanderers' 'He Banged the Leather for Goal', Portsmouth's take-up of the 'Pompey Chimes' (co-opted from Royal Artillery FC), and the adaptation of the music hall drinking song

'The Rowdy Dowdy Boys' by both Derby County and Sheffield United in the 1890s. Wolves' original anthem was written, almost unbelievably, by 'Pomp and Circumstance' classicist Sir Edward Elgar, long before 'Land of Hope and Glory' was being modified for the terraces. Elgar was known to cycle 40 miles from his home in Malvern to Molineux (and back), and was allegedly inspired to compose his proto-chant by striker Billy Malpass during a game between Wolves and Stoke City in February 1898. It was subsequently printed in *The Times*. However, unlike Norwich's anthem, Elgar's effort didn't reach the ears of the hoi polloi and was only rediscovered in 2010.

The singularity of 'On the Ball, City' extends to the fact that, despite sounding like a Pep Guardiola coaching mantra and despite all the other Cities in and outside the Football League, no club since has tried to appropriate it. Since the demise of their East Anglian precursors, it has been Norwich's alone. It even has its own page on the *Visit Norfolk* website. Yet does anybody outside of the county know the words? There's a 1959 piano-led recording credited to Norwich City FC, but the song has never come close to penetrating the charts and is not an ear-worm in the mould of some of our other entries. Indeed, even Norwich's own stand accused of not knowing the words and butchering Smith's magnum opus to the point that it's become indecipherable.

A song that the *Eastern Daily Press* once described as "the popular war cry of the clubbers" has had the equivalent of a 21st century club mix as modern fans have upped the tempo and mashed it up, leading to the *#slowdownOTBC* campaign. One supporter explained their preferred singing style via a classic rock analogy: "A bit more 'Stairway to Heaven' than 'White Riot'." Complaints about 'scrummage' displacing 'scrimmage' (a confused struggle) and a couple of erroneous 'it's (innocuously inserted between the original lyrics of 'kick off, throw in') may sound like material from an Alan Partridge radio phone-in, but the debate is no laughing matter to the Canaries. Even without anyone actively arguing its corner, modernism is winning this scrimmage, the march of progress trampling over tradition, which is a shame because 'On the Ball, City' is brimful of nostalgia and undoubtedly sounds better at a stately pace, as showcased by newsreel of supporters at the 1975 League Cup Final.

As with 'Bubbles', only the chorus is widely sung, which might go some way towards explaining the transition from pomp and grandeur to breakneck speed. The chorus speaks of 'a splendid rush', 'never mind the danger', 'Hurrah! We've scored a goal' — the match action crammed into a short stanza almost asking to be delivered in a frenetic burst. The opening lines, on the other hand, set a much more pensive tone:

> In the days to call, which we've left behind,
> Our boyhood's glorious game
> And our youthful vigour has declined.

While popular recordings of 'Bubbles' and 'Blue Moon' have gone harder and faster, 'On the Ball, City' could do with a balladeer to strip it back to its former glory. The mellifluous tones of celebrity fan and former club director Stephen Fry would be ideal. Fry has, in fact, posted a version from Songify (an app which turns spoken word into song), which is strangely redolent of an Oxbridge thespian crossed with Kanye West. All that's needed now is a historic accomplishment to mandate an official release.

Then again, starved of major honours, Norwich don't need too much excuse to issue a song. In both 1972 and 1982, tracks were recorded to commemorate being promoted back to the First Division. On the first occasion, as champions, the City squad got together with the Chic Applin Band to record 'The Canaries'. Songwriters Johnny Cleveland and Don Shepherd approached manager Ron Saunders with the idea. His response: "How much do we earn out of it?" Answer: not a lot. The sleeve notes were a tad optimistic in declaring, "the record has all the ingredients of a hit and there is no doubt that it will be accepted as the new Norwich City song to echo along the terraces". Peculiarly, the B-side has built a cult following who regularly champion it in fan votes for the Carrow Road walk-out music. In the days before cultural appropriation became offensive, 'Norwich City Calypso' brought an incongruous but beguiling cod-reggae vibe to the Norfolk coast. To wit (in Caribbean patois):

> Ron Saunders and his merry band
> Have brought the cheers from terrace and stand
> With scarfs, rosettes and rattles in hand
> They sing the Norwich City Calypso
>
> ...
>
> So our story now, it is almost done
> So thanks to the team for the victory won
> We will see you all in Division One
> Singing the Norwich City Calypso

Bob Marley famously liked his football and the creators of 'Norwich City Calypso', less famously, liked him right back, predating UB40 as the originators of white reggae by several years.

Finishing third in the Second Division, as Norwich did in 1982, is not much to shout about, but they did so anyway. 'Something to Shout About' feat. Accent (far less street than it sounds) is at least aware of its absurdity, built around the refrain, 'Who'd have thought those country boys would ever have something to shout about?' and namechecking future England goalkeeper Chris Woods as their regular saviour.

Indeed, who would even have dreamed of Division One in 1959, when Norwich were a third division outfit? Yet '59 was a year for dreaming, if you wore green and yellow. The Canaries finished fourth, narrowly missing out on promotion, and went on a fairytale cup run, beating Ilford, Swindon Town, Manchester United (3-0!), Cardiff City, Tottenham Hotspur and Sheffield United on their way to the FA Cup semi-final, where they were beaten by, of all people, Luton Town. A tear-jerking eulogy to their star strike partnership, 'The Ballad of Crossan and Bly' by Paul Wyett, appears on the 1999 club compilation *On the Ball City*, but wouldn't sound entirely out of place on *Five Leaves Left* or *John Wesley Harding*. Nick Drake and Bob Dylan would be proud of Wyett's wistful air and his socio-political pontificating in lines like these:

> You can keep your 4-2-4, your lying deep,
> your sponsored gear
> Your million-pound prima donnas
> in fancy shorts and puffed-up hair
> ...
> You can keep your coloured playback,
> electric scores in digital time
> I'll just have my memories of 1959

Running the full gamut of genres, *On the Ball City* (purists, please pardon the omission of the comma) also contains 'The Canary Rock 'N' Roll' by Gary Kennon, which channels the Seventies naff of Wizzard and the Rubettes. Apropos of nothing, Kennon released a whole album of Norwich-inspired songs, *Yellow and Green*, in early 2015. Maybe it inspired the Canaries to sing because they did proceed to get promoted again, triumphing in the play-offs.

What we really need, though, is a song to consecrate the Friendship Trophy. The what? Like rugby union's Calcutta Cup, the Friendship Trophy is open to only two teams: Norwich and Sunderland. It dates back to the 1985 League Cup Final, which was contested in such good spirits that it gave rise to its own prize, awarded to the winner each time the sides meet. On that inaugural occasion, Norwich took the Milk Cup thanks to an own goal by Gordon Chisholm. The jovial camaraderie was encapsulated by mingling on the London Underground afterwards; while Norwich fans sang 'we won the cup', the Mackems replied 'we scored the goal'! Here's an idea: leave the classics be and set that banter to a techno backing track instead.

Reviews

"If you have a spare sense of loyalty going, an impulse to follow without a special connection, then let me, in short, argue that you simply could not choose a more loveable and worthy club than Norwich City ... Should you, I repeat, have a spare shred of unattached allegiance in you, then why not affix it to the club that has the oldest song in footballing history?"

– Stephen Fry (taken from 'OTBC: An Open Letter to All Who Despise Sport', stephenfry.com, 13/08/11)

"I always feel like when Norwich do well, the Darkness does well. Last time they had a good run was when our first album came out. The first album was heavily influenced by East Anglia ... Ed Sheeran decided to set up an East Anglian derby. His team was Ipswich and the Darkness was Norwich. We won 7-5, but there exists a picture on my phone where we swapped shirts. Ed made me promise that nobody would ever see him in a Norwich shirt, so I'm going to blackmail him for a million quid!"

– Justin Hawkins, frontman of light-metal band the Darkness

"The Norwich crowd really doing all they can to lift their side, and I think they won that tackle for Jerry Goss!"

– commentator John Motson notes the impact of OTBC in the build-up to Jeremy Goss's eventual winner in the legendary 1993 UEFA Cup tie against Bayern Munich

"Forging memories through football is at the heart of Still On the Ball — an age UK Norwich group which brings older fans together and helps them unlock memories. Gathering in the 1959 Room of Norwich City Football Club a group of older fans, each living with dementia, and their carers, are getting ready to reminisce about legendary days gone by ... the theme from *Z-Cars* [is played] and the talk among the group turns to Everton."

– taken from an article in the *Eastern Daily Press* (2019) —
the group is at full capacity at the time of writing

6. The Blaydon Races

First released: c.1862
Highest UK chart position: N/A

St James' Park may as well be Newcastle Cathedral. Nowhere does the maxim that football is a religion ring truer than the North East. 'The Blaydon Races', though, is a permissive hymn to the local area that is far more colourful than black and white.

Taking in a day at the races on the other side of the Tyne, the song encompasses a rambunctious coach journey showcasing various real-life landmarks and characters, terminating at a rain and booze-soaked racetrack. The intermittent Blaydon festivities first took place in 1811, but were scrapped following a full-scale riot over the disqualification of a winning horse in 1916. A 1903 painting of the same name by William Irving depicts the Blaydon Races' bawdy carnival atmosphere in only a slightly more flattering light than William Hogarth's *Gin Lane*.

It was immortalised in song by a Tyneside music hall performer variously credited as George or Geordie Ridley. The etymology of the term 'Geordie' to refer to people from the vicinity of Newcastle is disputed. Some date it back to 1745 and the Jacobite rebellion, when the people of Newcastle and the surrounding area were said to be supporters of King George and Geordies became a derivation of Georges. Others link it to the local mining industry, either via the Geordie safety lamps designed by George Stephenson being favoured over the more common Davy lamps, or simply from George being a common name for pitmen in the North East.

Whatever the origin, George Ridley was Geordie through and through. He had been a trapper-boy from the age of eight, but turned to a career in music hall after being crushed by a wagon, an accident which left him unfit for manual labour. 'The Blaydon Races' was first performed at Balmbra's (as mentioned in its opening verse) in 1862 and was first published in George Ridley's *New Local Song Book*, probably the following year. Though popular in his time, that time was fleeting — he died in 1864 before his 30th birthday — and there was little indication that he would leave any sort of a legacy.

How exactly 'The Blaydon Races' came to be a terrace anthem and its creator memorialised in blue plaques across the city is unclear. Thomas Allan's *Tyneside Songs*, first published in the same year as George Ridley's *New Local Song Book* and expanded regularly for three decades thereafter, is sometimes credited with cementing it in the regional consciousness, but what elevates it above the other 400 folk songs collected? And why did the St James' Park faithful take it to their hearts?

The assimilation of an olde-worlde folk tune into 20th and 21st century football culture probably owes something to Newcastle's glory days belonging to the past. Their four league titles (1905, 1907, 1909 and 1927) and half of their FA Cup victories (1910, 1924 and 1932) are more closely aligned to the age of music hall than the age of recorded music. James Cosgrove, a singing comedian from Byker who performed under the name J. C. Scatter, made what is thought to be the first recording of 'The Blaydon Races' in the year of Newcastle's third league title, but radios and record players did not become standard household goods until the interwar years, so the song's spread owed more to oral transmission. One such form of transmission is communal gatherings, so it is possible that 'The Blaydon Races' was sung at St James' Park in these early days, but there seems to be no documentary evidence of that and it is instead thought to have first been sung at the 1924 FA Cup Final.

It had definitely been taken up by Newcastle's second prize-winning epoch of the 1950s, when they claimed a further three FA Cups. Programme notes from years later have the great Jackie Milburn (who netted a brace on the occasion under discussion) recalling a 6-1 demolition of Sunderland at Roker Park on Boxing Day, 1955:

> "Of course, the Sunderland supporters weren't as happy as ours but everybody stayed behind at the end and sang 'The Blaydon Races' together. There was a marvellous atmosphere with genuine comradeship. This was the North East together for Christmas, a sort of Geordie celebration and they made sure they enjoyed it — win or lose."

As affable as those Sunderland fans are coming across, it would typically be heresy to mix up Mackems (deriving from a shipbuilding phrase) and Geordies, yet 'The Blaydon Races' appears to have some currency on Wearside as well; it could apparently be heard during Sunderland's famous 1973 FA Cup victory but, as the dark days of hooliganism set in and the animosity between the rival regions deepened, it appears to have been jettisoned by those in red and white. Other clubs, including QPR, Walsall, Bolton Wanderers and Portadown FC have plagiarised it with their own geographical references, but none of the alternative versions have gained much traction. Not that there could be much grumbling from Geordies if they had: George Ridley set his own travelogue to a nicked tune titled 'On the Road to Brighton', though the Brighton in question was Boston, USA rather than 'and Hove Albion'.

Lee Hall, writer of the County Durham-set *Billy Elliot* — both film and musical — has written of Tyneside's folk song tradition that it was "so much part of the cultural furniture that I was not aware of its existence. Everybody I knew knew the same songs. In fact, everybody I knew had been sung the songs before they could speak, but somehow their ubiquity had made them invisible." He makes the case that 'The Blaydon Races' is more nursery rhyme than pop song, which might explain the lack of a definitive version. No recording has ever been remotely chart-bound and some of the more widely recognised ones, by folk acts such as the Spinners (Liverpool-based) and the Houghton Weavers (Greater Manchester), are understandably rejected on Tyneside in favour of the native opera bass Owen Brannigan's more overblown routine which was contemporaneous with Wor Jackie. The Animals' Eric Burdon was Ridley's great great nephew, but the Sixties beat combo responsible for 'The House of the Rising Sun' never honoured their heritage on record. *Auf Wiedersehen, Pet* trio Tim Healy, Jimmy Nail and Kevin Whately reunited in 2009 to record a specially-written verse for the recently deceased Sir Bobby Robson, but this failed to transfer to the terraces, which is less a reflection on the esteem in which the late Geordie legend is held than the fact that five of the previously existing six verses had already failed to make the cut in the communal consciousness of football fans, which tends to favour brevity. Should he release a live version from his homecoming gig at St James' Park on 9 June (symbolic for being the date that Ridley cites in his opening line) 2023, then youthful guitar hero Sam Fender could be the one to finally propel 'The Blaydon Races' into the charts.

It certainly requires a Geordie accent to do justice to the dialect in which it is written:

Aw went to Blaydon Races, 'twas on the ninth of Joon,
Eiteen hundred an' sixty-two on a summer's afternoon,
Aw tuek the bus frae Balmbra's, an' she wis heavy laden,
Away we went alang Collin'wood Street,
That's on the road to Blaydon
[Chorus]
O lads, ye shudda seen us gannin',

We passed the foaks alang the road just as they wor stannin';
Thor wes lots o' lads an' lasses there, all wi' smilling faces
Gan alang the Scotswood Road, to see the Blaydon Races

With an ear for proletarian vernacular and a painterly eye for social realism, Ridley is essentially a Victorian version of the Streets' Mike Skinner. Working-class larks and privations contrast with Newcastle's newfound status as the world's richest club, yet it could also be legitimately argued that the rich cultural heritage represented by 'The Blaydon Races' is more significant to the club's identity than Saudi Arabian riches. In a globalised market that increasingly detaches owners from fans and fans from community, ties that bind a club to the populus from which it first emerged are more precious than ever.

As with 'On the Ball, City', heritage value is evident in the consternation that it is not being sung correctly. Fanzine *The Mag* has complained of a bastardised version emanating from the stands and the engraving of the original lyrics into a redevelopment of the Bigg Market prompted debate over the evolution of certain words and phrases. But then the folk tradition has always worked like a broken telephone, distorted by misheard salvos and faulty memories. It is claimed that Thomas Allan's published versions sanitised 'The Blaydon Races' for the more respectable, musically trained middle-classes, so the 'wrong' words have been sung by many people since the 19th century, never mind the 21st. Another fan website publishes 'A Passable Version' that is intelligible to those not versed in the Geordie dialect but it's still written in rollicking non-standard English — really, it's the spirit that counts.

Back in 2017, with morale at a low ebb following the second relegation of the Mike Ashley regime, supporters group Wor Hyem 1892 coordinated a recording that aimed for an authentic match-day sound and a "tribal call to arms ahead of matches". Their efforts seemingly failed to satisfy fanzine *True Faith* (no known connection to the New Order song), which rejected 'The Blaydon Races' as a proper Newcastle United anthem when issuing a call for new walk-out music to ring in the Eddie Howe era. Suggestions included 'Big River' by Jimmy Nail, 'Waters of Tyne' by Sting, 'Fare Thee Well Northumberland' by Mark Knopfler, 'Geordie in Wonderland' by the Wildhearts, 'This Will Be Our Year' by the Zombies, and 'Hypersonic Missiles' and 'Saturday' by Sam Fender.

The glaring omission from the list, in the eyes of non-natives at least, is 'Fog on the Tyne (Revisited)' by Gazza and Lindisfarne. For the uninitiated, this number two hit from 1990 is probably more synonymous with Geordie life than 'The Blaydon Races'.

Newcastle heroes have a 'proud' pop tradition. Gazza followed the lead of Kevin Keegan ('Head Over Heels in Love', 1979, number 31) and Chris Waddle (Glenn and Chris — 'Diamond Lights', 1987, number 12) in launching a short-lived music career. Gazza-mania was at its peak after young Paul's performances and tears at Italia '90 endeared him to the nation, so the music industry saw an opportunity to cash-in. In Gascoigne's own words: "Somebody asked us if I wanted to do a record and I said I would do it."

The footballer-cum-pop-star featured on the covers of *Smash Hits* and *Melody Maker* to promote his debut single, which was a re-write of a song about life on the dole from Geordie folk-rockers Lindisfarne's number one album of the same name, originally released in 1971 and now enriched with a booming Nineties house beat and a rap referencing 'this Geordie boy' being 'spur[red] on in London town' when he heard those Geordies sing. The incongruity between genres echoes Gazza's own displacement from homespun Geordie lad to international megastar; the record tried to have its cake and eat it by representing him as the former while treating him as the latter. On Tottenham Hotspur's books after a then-British record transfer from Newcastle United in 1988, Gazza returned to the North East to film the music video on the banks of the Tyne with a host of star-struck hangers-on: according to an article in *Smash Hits*, there was "Gazza's family and Gazza's mates and Gazza's mates' mates and Gazza's mates' mates' second cousins".

The music press didn't regard Paul Gascoigne with the same affection as the general public and their generally scathing reportage precipitated a media backlash and the unravelling of the Gazza persona. As the Charlatans' Tim Burgess observed in a parallel interview with *Smash Hits*:

> "I think he's being manipulated. I think it's a real shame. Would you risk your character, your individualism for that? The press are manipulating him to a massive degree and I think that's diabolical. He should stick to doing his own bloody thing."

Follow-up single 'Geordie Boys (Gazza Rap)' stalled at number 31 and the album *Let's Have a Party* (featuring a cover of 'All You Need is Love' and Jive Bunny-style medleys of Elvis, Motown, disco and Gilbert O'Sullivan) disappeared without trace. A short time after his music career wound down, Gazza got wound up in the 1991 FA Cup Final and ruptured a cruciate ligament throwing himself into a horror tackle on Gary Charles. The injury, exacerbated by an incident in a Tyneside nightclub, kept him out for the entirety of the 1991-92 season and he became a fixture on the front pages rather than the back, even when he was once again able to grace the pitch with his talents (see the fluting during his Rangers days, which was probably more ill-advised than any other musical exploit).

If a music career left Gazza as confounded as those on the coach to Blaydon, 'Fog on the Tyne (Revisited)' also took its toll on Lindisfarne. Joint lead vocalist Ray Jackson departed after refusing to take part in the video shoot or a *Top of the Pops* appearance: "I felt we were selling out; the rest of the band disagreed. Gazza was a great footballer and a Geordie hero but no musician. I similarly could never play football."

Reviews

"What is a club, in any case? Not the buildings or the directors or the people who are paid to represent it... It's the noise, the passion, the feeling of belonging, the pride in your city."

– Sir Bobby Robson in his autobiography, *Newcastle: My Kind of Toon* (2008)

"That buzz when you walk out at St James' is special. I never really used to hear the singing on the pitch during the game; when you walked out the atmosphere was loud and that's when I used to soak it all in... 'The Blaydon Races' is an iconic song if you are from Newcastle. Certainly, the local lads understand what it is, but trying to get the foreign lads to understand the words is difficult. I know a verse or two, but don't ask me to sing the whole thing."

– record goalscorer Alan Shearer, who unveiled a train named 'Blaydon Races' to celebrate 150 years of the Geordie anthem in 2012, and sang it ringside when lightweight Lewis Ritson fought at Newcastle's Metro Radio Arena in 2018

"Sam Fender, at St James' Park on Blaydon races day, with Wor Flags undoubtedly adding to the spectacle. Just need a Greggs pastie and a brown ale with every ticket and you've got the most Geordie day imaginable."

– Jamie Smith writing for *The Mag* (NUFC's largest independent fan site) in 2022

"It is one of the great symbols of the North East — along with the Tyne Bridge, Angel of the North and St James' Park — considered sacrosanct by people with a deep sense of belonging and genuine pride in their community."

– Christopher Hoy, *The Guardian* (2012)

7. Blue is the Colour

First released: 1972
Highest UK chart position: 5

Despite the King's Road's reputation for opulence, they're simple souls at heart in west London. Take Mickey Greenaway, aka the Zigger-Zagger Man. This larger-than-life legend of Stamford Bridge is reputed to have been behind the Fulham Road Stand's re-christening as the Shed; its low roof, originally designed to protect greyhound punters from the elements, provided the best acoustics for his booming voice and the 'Shed End' was therefore where Chelsea's most vocal followers were urged to congregate. Greenaway (b.1945; d.1999) was responsible for the nonsensical chant 'Zigger-zagger, zigger-zagger, oi oi oi!' (later reworked into the Spice Girls' breakout hit) and the Bridge's uptake of 'One Man Went to Mow', which inexplicably snuck onto a mixtape he'd taken on a pre-season tour of Sweden in 1981 and stuck after it tickled the Blues fans pink.

Greenaway didn't write 'Blue is the Colour', but his musical influence is implied in the line 'Come to the Shed and we'll welcome you'. The team behind the song were more professional than the

Zigger-Zagger Man, but not as well-versed in club tradition. Songwriters Daniel Boone and Rod McQueen, who had just had a worldwide hit with 'Beautiful Sunday', were the men tasked with composing a Chelsea-inspired song in time for the 1972 League Cup Final. The problem was, they knew their way around a recording studio, but not a football pitch. Producer Larry Page, who released the record on his own Penny Farthing imprint, had been involved with Chelsea since the mid-Sixties, when the worlds of music and football collided and players such as Terry Venables and George Graham were hanging out at his office with rock stars such as the Kinks and the Troggs. Page recalls having to talk Boone and McQueen through the basics:

> "I ended up making a list of things that actually happened at the games and how people enjoyed it, telling them about things like the Shed and 'down at the Bridge', and the fact that it was all so blue, and that's how it started to come together."

'Blue is the colour' is, then, a simple statement of fact rather than a knowledgeable reference to the club's changing hues, from the paler Eton blue taken from the horse racing colours of Lord Chelsea, who was then club president, to the more familiar royal blue shirts that have been worn since 1912. Similarly, 'Chelsea is our name' is a boast that is entirely ignorant of the fact that Fulham, the London borough in which Chelsea FC is located, was already taken and the name of the neighbouring borough was only settled on after London FC, Kensington FC and Stamford Bridge FC had been rejected. The song is essentially *Chelsea for Dummies*, but therein lies its charm. As Bill Shankly said, "Football is a simple game made complicated by people who should know better." The songwriters of 'Blue is the Colour' didn't know any better and so it communicates — by necessity rather than intricate design — the essence of Chelsea FC in the most digestible and relatable way, which is paradoxically what makes it so special.

And there is a minimalist harmony between the artless lyrics and the oompah brass backing track. At a time when others were beginning to go disco, Chelsea won out with a marching band arrangement that wouldn't have been out of place half a century earlier and retains its timeless quality more than half a century on. The song's universal appeal is borne out by its army of translations. Within a year of release it had been modified by Ajax ('Ajax, Leve Ajax!' reached number 25 in the Dutch charts), Marseille, the Danish national team and the Australian cricket team ('Here Come the Aussies', for the 1972 Ashes series). A September 1972 issue of *Billboard* magazine carried the headline "British Soccer Team Song Breaks Globally" and reported that worldwide sales were already approaching one million. To put that into context, the UK's biggest-selling single of 1972 — 'Amazing Grace' by the Royal Scots Dragoon Guards — racked up sales of 890,000. This simple, unassuming song has somehow traversed oceans, colours, sports and politics. Other notable versions include Scottish duo the Proclaimers being enlisted to record 'White is the Colour' for the Vancouver Whitecaps and the Conservatives using it as the basis for their successful 1979 election campaign: 'Blue is the colour / Maggie is her name...'! It is unclear whether Thatcher approved given her pronounced distaste for the national game and its followers.

The original recording session certainly didn't hint at global domination. The Chelsea squad had been given cassettes to help them learn the lyrics in advance but Page recalls there being little evidence of homework having been completed. There had, however, been a different form of preparation: according to midfielder Tommy Baldwin's account, "about ten cases of lager and a couple of cases of vodka" had been procured "to help ease the nerves". Some players, it seems, were more scared of the microphone than opponents were of Ron 'Chopper' Harris. Teetotal right-back Paddy Mulligan says that those who mixed the record are due a lot of credit for making the lads sound sober, never mind in tune. An unsteady foundation of copious alcohol consumption also underpinned the squad's appearance on *Top of the Pops* when 'Blue is the Colour' infiltrated the higher reaches of the charts, though the UK's premier music show mercifully stipulated lip-syncing rather than a live vocal performance. The recording session was actually well-oiled enough that it garnered a full album's worth of material, though there was little danger of *Top of the Pops* inviting Peter Osgood back to do 'Chirpy Chirpy Cheep Cheep' or David Webb to sing 'Alouette' (so unconventional that the defender merits an arrangement credit on the traditional French-language children's song).

It may have proven popular but 'Blue is the Colour' perhaps didn't provide the ideal preparation for the League Cup final. Chelsea were riding the crest of a wave and were firm favourites, having won their first FA Cup in 1970 and beaten Real Madrid to the European Cup Winners' Cup in 1971. But on the day they were beaten 2-1 by Stoke City. It is fortunate that the lyricists made no cocksure reference to the club's recent glory and instead alluded to mixed fortunes and the need to 'cheer us on through sun and rain', because the anthem ushered in a barren quarter-century until Chelsea's Nineties reinvention.

Just as Britpop harked back to bygone glories, the Chelsea of the mid-Nineties began to recapture the panache of the Sixties and Seventies, albeit with a more cosmopolitan bent. Following the international assembly of Vialli, Zola and Leboeuf, following Chelsea became a hipsterish pursuit. Blur frontman Damon Albarn developed an intense affiliation which appeared to have been long forgotten until Britpop rivalries were reignited in the aftermath of the 2021 Champions League Final between Chelsea and Manchester City, when a despondent Noel Gallagher bumped into a victorious Albarn among the corporate loungers and impolitely asked his nemesis to "fuck off". Damon was joined at Stamford Bridge in the Nineties by his 'Parklife' chum Phil Daniels, *Fantasy Football League*'s David Baddiel, *Soccer AM*'s Tim Lovejoy and, breaking ranks from his hometown allegiance to Glasgow Rangers and his high-profile Mancunian signings, Creation Records supremo Alan McGee.

Also watching from the sidelines was Graham McPherson, better known by his stage name Suggs, lead singer of ska revivalists

Madness. "When I was kid," Suggs writes in the foreword to *Blue Day — Wembley '97: The Heroes' Stories*, "I wanted to be Chelsea's centre-forward... but that was never going to happen. 'Blue Day' was the next best thing for me." By which he means the song the book shares its title with.

Written by Mike Connaris, 'Blue Day' combines a classic Beatles chord progression with the cynical optimism of 'Three Lions' — lyrics like 'We've waited so long, but we'd wait forever' make 'Blue is the Colour' and 'Blue Day' the bookends of Chelsea's trophy drought, which Roberto Di Matteo and co. brought to an end, while Roman Abramovich's roubles, since replaced by Todd Boehly's largesse, have made a return to such barren times unlikely. The real driving force behind 'Blue Day', however, was Barbara Charone, an American lady in the Warner Bros press department who got hold of Connaris's demo and enthusiastically badgered Suggs into fronting a cup final song with the squad providing backing vocals, which he feared was going to be "naff". Suggs also credits her with being the most fanatical Chelsea supporter he's ever met, though it's unknown if he ever met Mickey Greenaway, who was fingered (many say erroneously) as "King of the Soccer Hooligans" by the Sunday tabloids and became a recluse throughout the Nineties. One hopes Greenaway was sat in front of the TV singing 'Zigger-Zagger' as the boys of '97 beat Middlesbrough; he wouldn't live to see Chelsea lift the Premier League or the Champions League trophies. Nor did he get to see them return to *Top of the Pops*; manager Ruud Gullit, perhaps conscious of what went on in 1972, wisely vetoed a pre-match performance as 'Blue Day' climbed to number 22 in the charts.

It was, however, played by the Wembley DJ at the final whistle, with 'Blue is the Colour' sandwiched between another play. Then another. And another. Suggs describes it as "one of the highlights of my entire life — one of those moments when you can't imagine anything getting any better. It was euphoric, up there with some of the greatest things I'd ever done with Madness. It's only if you're a football fan that you realise the enormity of these things."

Reviews

"The British public are very tolerant but we couldn't believe it ourselves when it got to number five. I knew I couldn't sing anyway but the lads who were drinking were trying to camouflage the fact that they couldn't sing and it just got worse. I said to Ron Harris, 'now don't kick the microphone Ron, whatever you do!' We were causing all sorts of trouble but we had a smashing day."

– the memories of Paddy Mulligan, who played for Chelsea between 1969 and 1972

"The Chelsea boys did it in style. It was catchy and original, and for a football team song it was a different class."

– late, great Chelsea and England forward Peter Osgood in his autobiography *Ossie: King of Stamford Bridge* (2002)

"Favourite colour? Blue, Chelsea blue."

– Tim Lovejoy, presenter of Sky Sports' madcap magazine show *Soccer AM*

"A great song is a great song in its simplest form. These guys knew that."

– Mike Connaris, composer of *Blue Day*

8. Leeds! Leeds! Leeds! (Marching on Together)

First released: 1972
Highest UK chart position: 10

They're a different breed in West Yorkshire. Google 'what does mot stand for' and you'll get pages of information about motoring and transport. Google 'what does mot stand for leeds' and the top hit tells you that it's an acronym of allegiance, standing for 'marching on together', which is the name of the club anthem. Only — technically speaking — Leeds have never had a song called 'Marching on Together'.

Back in 1972 — a vintage year for cup songs — Leeds United FC released the imaginatively titled 'Leeds United' to mark their appearance in the centenary FA Cup Final. It was essentially a roll call of star players and their attributes, like a team version of 'The Ballad of Billy Bremner', which had been released the previous year by Ronnie Hilton, but failed to recapture the chart success that the Yorkshire crooner had enjoyed between the mid-Fifties and mid-Sixties.

Surprisingly, there is a hat-trick of songs titled 'Leeds United', and the other two are probably better known among music aficionados.

Professional malcontent Luke Haines (formerly of the Auteurs and Black Box Recorder) released it as the lead track of the *Leeds United EP* in 2007, in which he uses football as a metaphor for police failings in the case of 'Yorkshire Ripper' Peter Sutcliffe ('It's a 13-0 defeat' refers to the body count rather than a club record loss) and for the general malaise that suffocated the 1970s.

Slightly more upbeat is the 2008 single by Amanda Palmer, half of 'Brechtian punk cabaret' duo the Dresden Dolls, taken from her first solo album, *Who Killed Amanda Palmer?*. Why would a Boston chanteuse be singing about Leeds United? Having briefly dated Ricky Wilson of the Kaiser Chiefs (responsible for terrace-friendly anthems such as 'I Predict a Riot' and 'Ruby', and named after the club that defensive stalwart Lucas Radebe was bought from), she was gifted a Leeds United jersey after a stopover in his home city and subsequently lost it on tour: 'I had that shirt for all of about five days. I'd already gotten all excited and sentimental about it, and then it vanished.' Having lost her wallet, keys and all manner of other shit around the same time, Palmer poured her frustrations into song:

> "I loved the words 'Leeds United'. It's such a sexy name for a team, and there's something so great and military and bold sounding about that *united*, Leeds *United* ... 'Leeds United' was going to be this really ironic bold united statement, where everything was falling apart."

The perfect anthem then for the Peter Ridsdale era, when the high-flying Leeds imploded and the chairman's expensive goldfish became as symbolic of a failed regime as Imelda Marcos's shoe collection.

Though barely known today, the club's own 'Leeds United' out-performed indie darlings Haines and Palmer commercially, spending ten weeks in the top 75 and peaking at number ten. To still be selling copies in July, two months after a day in the Wembley sun, is impressive staying power for an FA Cup song. However, as the A-side fell by the wayside, it was the B-side — 'Leeds! Leeds! Leeds!' — which demonstrated true longevity. While the A-side was specific to Don Revie's cup-winning team, the B-side — better known by its 'marching on together' refrain — speaks for the soul of its club: the supporters.

Written in the first-person plural, every 'we love', 'we shout' and 'we're gonna' hardens the effect of communion that is inherent in any tribal allegiance. It has been routinely played before kick-off for quite some time, its constancy matching that of fans, although there is a theory that the song migrated from Elland Road to Headingley when disenchanted football fans went to watch the Leeds Rhinos instead. Contrary to the 'marching on together' lyrics, it aggravates some Leeds United ultras that their anthem has been hijacked by rugby league, and the feelings of covetousness are not aided by hearsay that the Rhinos bought the sound recording rights when the city's football club went into receivership!

As the song states, 'we've had our ups and downs (ups and downs)'. Some appreciate the supporter-added '(ups and downs)' echo, some don't. As per tradition, the substitution of 'na na na' for handclaps is also a source of controversy. What is indisputable is that 'Leeds! Leeds! Leeds! (Marching on Together)' has remained popular through highs and lows. In fact, a remastered version from 2010, credited to Leeds United Team and Supporters and released in celebration of promotion from League One back to the Championship (less than a decade after reaching a Champions League semi-final), matched the original by reaching the top 10. True to form, it then plummeted to 112 — the second largest drop in UK singles chart history. A beautifully understated version by local band Shadowlark was also used on *Take Us Home*, the Amazon Prime documentary that charted Andrea Radrizzani and Marcelo Bielsa's eventually successful attempts to return a fallen giant to the promised land of the Premier League.

The other most striking thing about Leeds' 1972 cup songs is that they were composed by Ivor Novello Award-winning songwriters Les Reed and Barry Mason, who were also responsible for Stoke City's anthem of choice, 'Delilah'. However, whereas Reed and Mason were commissioned to write 'Leeds United' and 'Leeds!

Leeds! Leeds!', 'Delilah' was intended for Tom Jones alone and only entered footballing folklore through dumb luck. There are competing theories as to how it made its way to the Potteries, some less dumb than others.

The first involves a gig by the Sensational Alex Harvey Band at the old Victoria Ground on 17 May 1975, at which their cover of 'Delilah' was so well received that its singing at the football was a hangover from those who were in attendance. The problems with this theory are manifold: (1) the headliners on the night were prog rockers Yes and it is rare for a support act to steal the show, although memories from myvintagerock.com attest that they did, and the unverified recollection of a mass kickabout between sets reinforces the footballing link; (2) anecdotes say there was a match the next day, which seems quite an undertaking to dismantle the stage for what would have been a meaningless May friendly, and it would have had to be quite some performance from the Sensational Alex Harvey Band for 'Delilah' to have been rehashed when Stoke opened their league season with a home defeat to West Ham on 16 August; (3) there is scant evidence of 'Delilah' being sung on the terraces before the late-Eighties.

The second theory sounds far-fetched, but is perhaps more credible. Anton Booth, owner of Newcastle-under-Lyme roofing firm A.D. Booth and Sons, but curiously known as TJ among Stoke supporters, told the *Stoke Sentinel* in 2009 that it all began at an away fixture to Derby in 1987: "We were all in a pub and the police asked us not to sing a song with swear words on. So we put 'Delilah' on the jukebox, and I got up on a table and started singing it. We sang it in the ground and it just went from there." Appeasing a police request for civility with a song about infidelity and domestic violence would certainly appeal to the dark humour of most travelling fans, and a third theory attributes the song to Stoke's dire time in the third tier at the turn of the Nineties, when disgruntled fans exiting the stadium would change the lyrics to 'So before they come to open the door / Forgive me Stoke City, I just couldn't take any more'.

The late Barry Mason once said of 'Delilah', "It is a drinking song really, you need a pint in one hand and a scarf in the other." The same could be said of 'Leeds! Leeds! Leeds! (Marching on Together)' except it has the added advantage of chronicling communal passion rather than a crime of passion and leads to triumph rather than murder!

Reviews

"A rousing, almost arousing, paean to Leeds United ... its blend of jauntiness and faux militaristic bombast melodically captur[es] the power of a crowd mobilised in the name of fun and communal pride."

– Paul Doyle, football writer for *The Guardian*

"It's never easy to be a Leeds fan. The pressure from the entire city behind the team — that's hard but it also has a positive factor."

– Simon Rix, Kaiser Chief's bassist and president of the Leeds United Supporters' Trust since 2019

"[Before the game,] 'Marching on Together' started up from the tannoy. I watched the pure joy as [club legend] Eddie Gray stopped to take in the atmosphere, belting out the words with a huge grin on his face, pumping his fists and clapping his hands to the fans, looking like he was enjoying singing that song more than anyone I've ever seen."

– 'Where there's hope there's Eddie Gray', written by Rob Conlon and published in fanzine *The Square Ball*, 17 May 2022

"Football is art. It's live theatre, it's passionate and emotional, people care a lot about it. It'd been a rollercoaster of a season and when we didn't quite make promotion it felt like the documentary, that was so dramatic and emotionally charged, needed the soundtrack to match. Obviously the original 'Marching on Together' is pretty 'jovial' sounding. I wanted to make our version beautiful and juxtapose it to match the mood. I think a lot of people connected with it at the time and they've since told me they play it at weddings and funerals — which is very Leeds. MOT."

– Ellen Smith, lead singer and songwriter with Shadowlark

"Our two founders still tease each other over who came up with the idea for the group name! It's a perfect fit though, and the anthem captures the sense of fellowship all football fans feel when going to a match. We strongly promote the message that football is for everyone, so the emphasis on marching on — and out — together is a key theme, and the line 'we are so proud' also resonates especially deeply for us."

– Marching Out Together, Leeds United's LGBT+ group

9. Theme from Z-Cars

First released: 1962
Highest UK chart position: 8

What is a Z-car (pronounced 'zed')? The Ford Zephyr was the standard police patrol car used by forces across the UK, while the Ford Zodiac was used for specialist tasks, such as traffic duty, so Z-car became an idiom for police vehicles until the Ford Anglia 'panda' car became the more prominent model. It also refers to the radio call signals used by the Lancashire Constabulary, with different divisions assigned different letters and Z being allocated to the fictional territory of Newtown, which was the setting for the BBC's ground-breaking TV show *Z-Cars*.

The theme tune to *Z-Cars* was heard twice-weekly on BBC1 from 1962 to 1978, discounting a brief interlude between 1965 and 1967 when the show was replaced by a spin-off and various unsuccessful soap operas before being brought back by popular demand. (One of its replacements — *United!* — followed the fortunes of a fictional second division football team named Brentwich United, counted Jimmy Hill as a technical advisor and was filmed on the grounds of

Stoke City.) Twelve series and 801 episodes is a pretty long stretch, yet the theme tune can still be heard several decades later at both Goodison Park and Vicarage Road. Watford began playing it for no other reason than manager Bill McGarry liked it, and it fast became a good luck charm; it was introduced after a home defeat to Peterborough in October 1963 and the home team wouldn't taste defeat again until December 1964, 29 matches later. However, it counts as Everton's anthem first and foremost because its origins are more closely tied to the locale, it was heard at Goodison slightly earlier (indeed, one of the reasons McGarry is said to have liked it was because he sought to emulate Harry Catterick's Everton) and it has been used even more steadfastly (Watford swapped for Elton John's 'I'm Still Standing' in 2019 — though their former owner was honourably invited to select one of his songs, the change was not at his behest and fans successfully petitioned the Pozzo family to bring back 'Z-Cars' in time for Christmas 2020; Elton's choice may or may not have been ironically intended but its short reign spanned four separate managers, excluding Hayden Mullins' two stints as caretaker).

Z-Cars first aired on 2 January 1962 and two versions of its theme tune hit the charts two months later. The one by Scottish multi-instrumentalist Johnny Keating fared best (it reached number eight) and remains the most widely heard. It was provided with competition by Norrie Paramor and his Orchestra, who stalled at number 33. A third version, containing vocals by cast member James Ellis, failed to chart. There have been a few aborted attempts by fans to fit words to the melody, typically in honour of favourite players, but such exercises are generally deemed unnecessary and the song best left alone or just hummed along to, like the sound of a revving engine.

The lyrics used by Ellis were the words to the folk song 'Johnny Todd', which 'Theme from Z-Cars' is sometimes known as because it was this traditional tune that was given the TV treatment by husband-and-wife arrangers Fritz Spiegl and Bridget Fry. Also in

1962, 'Johnny Todd' featured on *Quayside Songs Old and New* by Liverpudlian folk quartet the Spinners, and in 1967 it was laid down by Bob Dylan and the Band, but their home recording didn't see the light of day until the release of *The Bootleg Series Vol. 11: The Basement Tapes Complete* in 2014. Long before Dylan sang of the eponymous cuckolded sailor, Todd's tale appeared in *Traditional Tunes: A Collection of Ballad Airs* (1891), in which the curator Frank Kidson noted, "'Johnny Todd' is a child's rhyme, heard and seen played by Liverpool children".

This local connection is presumably why it was translated to *Z-Cars*. Though the setting of Newtown was fictional, the programme was based on and filmed in the Mersey suburb of Kirkby (historically part of Lancashire). The northern realism of *Z-Cars* contrasted heavily with much of the BBC's plummy output, its strong regional flavour giving it more in common with *EastEnders* than *Dixon of Dock Green*. That said, in a cast including Brian Blessed, Leonard Rossiter, John Thaw and future Monkee Davy Jones, there was only one native Liverpudlian: Leonard Williams, who played Sgt. Percy Twentyman.

Leonard Williams' connection to Everton playing 'Theme from Z-Cars' is a matter of some conjecture. What's certain is that it began as early as the 1962-63 title-winning season. In this context, as with Gerry and the Pacemakers coinciding with Liverpool's league triumph the following season, it's easy to see why it endured. (Local bragging rights to Everton for their anthem pre-dating Liverpool's; 'You'll Never Walk Alone' was actually released in the very same month that Watford appropriated 'Theme from Z-Cars'.) Accepted wisdom is to print the legend and the well-trodden tale is that the theme song debuted at Goodison Park when Williams brought some of the cast and crew along to watch the 5-0 trouncing of Blackpool on 10 November 1962. A few days later, Williams' life was cut tragically short by a heart attack (he was 48 years old) and the playing of 'Theme from Z-Cars' was dedicated to him in memoriam. However, a local historian who has scoured the archives of the *Liverpool Echo* found reference to the theme being 'played for the first seven or eight home matches' and then strangely 'left out on the very day the late Mr Leonard Williams of Twentyman fame was a guest of the club'. Columnist Leslie Edwards wrote:

> "The club say there was no official adoption of the tune and that it has not been stopped for any special reason. As one who counted Twentyman and his Liverpudlian cracks as the most authoritative mirror of football fans in this city, it mightn't be a bad idea to adopt the *Z-Cars* drums and fifes and commemorate one of the city's notable sons."

Funky fact: should Edwards' suggestion have been the stimulus for the tune's resurrection at the start of the 1963-64 season then that makes two significant contributions to Merseyside football folklore from two generations of the same family; it was Leslie's father, the *Echo*'s sports editor Ernest Edwards, who in 1906 christened the Kop after comparing Anfield's new mount of terracing to the notorious South African hill Spioenkop, which had been the site of a Boer War massacre involving the Lancashire Fusiliers in 1900.

Everton's usage of the theme rumbled into the public consciousness at the 1963 Charity Shield, a 4-0 thumping of Manchester United. Under the headline "The Last Word by J. L. Manning — a Z-Car Named Desire", the *Daily Mail*'s correspondent reported that "Televiewers must have crashed from their armchairs during the ill-tempered charity match amid the rowdies of Liverpool when the commentator suddenly announced Everton's new victory march." And the Toffees have stuck with it ever since, bar an ill-advised dalliance with the classical strains of Richard Strauss ('Also sprach Zarathustra' — theme from *2001: A Space Odyssey*) and Aaron Copland ('Fanfare for the Common Man') in 1994. New chairman Peter Johnson was reportedly the instigator of the bid to go highbrow, but he was set straight by former player Joe Royle when he returned as manager in November that year.

Sunderland did successfully ditch 'Theme from Z-Cars' (played at Roker Park in the Seventies and Eighties, nobody really knows why) for Sergei Prokofiev's stirring 'Dance of the Knights' when they moved to the Stadium of Light but, just as 'Bubbles' and 'Blaydon Races' keep upwardly mobile clubs connected to their working-class roots, it is virtually guaranteed that 'Z-Cars' will follow Everton to Bramley-Moore Dock. When the club pretended that the anthem was to be replaced on April Fool's Day 2005, supporters did not find the joke funny.

Its instrumental status perhaps precludes it from being covered by the playing squad, so Everton FC has never issued its own version of the theme, though affiliates have mixed it up a bit. The 'Call to Arms 97 Version' by Blueknowz was stocked by the Everton Megastore. And boxer Tony Bellew, who won the WBC cruiserweight title at Goodison Park in 2016, overdubbed sirens to his team's anthem to spice up his ring-walk; the dramatic effect was duly retained for matchdays, save for the visit of Manchester City on 26 February 2022 when, in light of Russia's invasion of Ukraine two days earlier, sirens were deemed insensitive and Goodison staged a show of support for the traumatised Ukrainians on opposing sides (Everton's January signing Vitalii Mykolenko and City's Oleksandr Zinchenko).

Wartime spirit infuses some of Everton's other terrace anthems. 'All Together Now' was a hit for scally-baggys the Farm in 1990, whose founder Peter Hooton had also launched the football fanzine *The End* in 1981, which evolved out of punk's DIY, anti-establishment ethos. In *The Football Imagination* (1995), Richard Haynes ascribes the rise of fanzines to a desire to voice an alternative view of football, combating the mainstream media's portrait of fans as thugs. The Farm's involvement in the game certainly rises to these objectives. The band had been central to 'The Fields of Anfield Road', released as a fundraiser for the victims of Hillsborough and credited to the Liverpool Collective featuring the Kop Choir. As part of the Hillsborough Justice Campaign they also played a 'Don't Buy the Sun' concert in 2011, in continued protest at the tabloid newspaper's false reporting of the disaster, and formed the core of the Justice Collective, who claimed the Christmas number one in 2012 with their cover of 'He Ain't Heavy, He's My Brother', inspired by Everton's own Hillsborough tribute which included a pre-match playing of the Hollies' version. While taking the fight to social injustice, further evidence of the Farm peacefully crossing the Mersey divide is there in Everton's re-working of 'All Together Now' for the 1995 FA Cup Final. Originally written about the Christmas truce kickabout between British and German soldiers in 1914, the chorus was changed from 'all together now / in no man's land' to 'all together now / for Everton'. The melody lends itself to a football chant and is still sung today, as well as having been revamped by DJ Spoony for Euro 2004.

'It's a Grand Old Team to Play For' is also second-hand, believed to have originated with Belfast Celtic in the 1920s and made famous by Glasgow Celtic, while owing a lot to 'With Cat-Like Tread' from Gilbert and Sullivan's 1879 comic opera the *Pirates of Penzance.* Every team adapts it accordingly and, where the Farm sought to heal rifts, Everton's lyrics to 'Grand Old Team' only serve to inflame hostilities with reference to 'the Red sh*te'.

The rivalry between Blues and Reds could make 'You'll Never Walk Alone' topping another chart from 2021 a bitter pill to swallow for Evertonians, were it not for the fact that 'Theme from Z-Cars' is the unlikely occupier of fourth spot and the polling equivalent of a Champions League place. The top ten in full:

1. You'll Never Walk Alone
2. The Chain
3. Soul Limbo
4. Theme from Z-Cars
5. Match of the Day Theme
6. Swing Low Sweet Chariot
7. Blue Moon
8. I'm Forever Blowing Bubbles
9. Marching on Together
10. Blue is the Colour

And the subject of the poll? The most popular sports-related funeral songs, conducted by Co-Op Funeralcare. The School of Science correctly identified 'Theme from Z-Cars' as top-notch entrance music; turns out it's highly prized as exit music too.

Reviews

"'Z-Cars' started playing on the PA and I heard the crowd roar. If I could bottle a moment and save it forever, then that'd be it."

– Alan Harper, a Liverpudlian full-back who had two spells at Everton (1983-88 and 1991-93)

"The most important record of all ... If you want to see Bill Kenwright at his happiest, at his most content, you'll see him as Everton kick off."

– the late Everton chairman Bill Kenwright, speaking on *Desert Island Discs* in 1998

"Keating felt that the 'Theme from Z-Cars' had become the 'Everton Theme' at no extra cost to the Toffees. He'd like to meet to discuss the re-arrangement of — and royalties from — the 'Theme from Z-Cars'... nice chap — a bit serious but clearly proud of his place in classical music."

– David Exall, club promotions manager in the 1960s-70s, as told to ToffeeWeb

"Z Cars just hits different."

– Everton official Twitter account, 23 October 2022

10. Ossie's Dream (Spurs Are on Their Way to Wembley)

First released: 1981
Highest UK chart position: 5

We're off to Wembley 'cos we beat the Arsenal
We're off to Wembley 'cos we beat the Arsenal
In the North London Cup, they was only runners-up
And they can't get the double up the Arsenal

Chas & Dave's 'The Victory Song (We're Off to Wembley 'Cos We Beat the Arsenal)' from 1991 mercilessly mocks the Gunners, but the Rockney duo's cottage industry writing cup songs for their beloved Tottenham Hotspur owes more than they'd care to admit to their north London neighbours.

'The Angel (North London Forever)', by Louis Dunford, son of *Birds of a Feather*'s Linda Robson, is a love song to Islington that has recently planted a red and white flag in the north London turf, conveniently ignoring Arsenal's Woolwich origins. It was largely ignored on its spring '22 release but within a few months had infiltrated the Emirates, aided and abetted by social media and Amazon's *All or Nothing* documentary. As with its chief cheerleader,

Mikel Arteta, who invited Dunford to the training ground, only time will tell if it's the real deal or a jumped-up pretender, but its terrace adoption shows that the folk instinct is intact. Still, 'One-nil to the Ar-se-nal' remains probably the best-known song to come out of Highbury or the Emirates Stadium, much better known than official Arsenal FC releases such as 'We're Back Where We Belong' (1989 — sounds like something from an Eighties rom-com), 'Shouting for the Gunners' (1993 — Brixton reggae singer Tippa Irie gets a muted reception from the Highbury library), 'Hot Stuff' (1998 — a travesty of a Donna Summer cover that only Ian Wright could be enthusiastic about) and 'Arsenal Number One/Our Goal' (2000 — makes Lou Bega's 'Mambo No. 5' sound sophisticated, backed by an *X Factor* reject track). Their trademark chant — to the tune of 'Go West' by the Village People (1979) and covered by the Pet Shop Boys (1993), itself based on Johann Pachelbel's 'Canon in D' from 1680 — began during a European Cup Winners' Cup semi-final at the Parc des Princes in 1994 as a means of goading the Boulogne Boys, the PSG ultras who had already set 'Allez, Paris Saint-Germain' to the same strain. Eulogising this classic scoreline was an accurate homage to the tactical dogma of George Graham, and continued to be sung with ironic gusto during the more swashbuckling tenure of Arsène Wenger. However, it's the less celebrated but historically significant 'Good Old Arsenal' that pianist Charles Nicholas Hodges and bassist David Victor Peacock owe a sizeable chunk of their fame and fortune to.

The Sixties pop explosion had clearly had an impact on football culture, but it took visionary pundit Jimmy Hill — already responsible for the abolition of the maximum wage during his stint playing for Fulham and chairing the Professional Footballers' Association — to identify the commercial opportunities of combining cup and chart success. En route to their first ever league and FA Cup double in 1970-71 (only the fourth ever and the first since Tottenham had achieved it a decade earlier), Arsenal were encouraged by Hill to find a club anthem to rival Liverpool's 'You'll Never Walk Alone', but to make it an original composition rather than steal from the pop charts. Pre-empting *Pop Idol* by three decades, wannabe musicians were invited to enter their songs into an ITV competition. The winner, bizarrely, was Hill! With none of the submissions deemed adequate, this Seventies Renaissance man put down his *Big Match* microphone to pen his own anthem, under the patronage of Arsenal manager Bertie Mee. The result was 'Good Old Arsenal', to the tune of 'Rule, Britannia!' ('Good old Arsenal / We're proud to say that name / And while we sing this song / We'll win the game'). Recorded by the Arsenal First Team Squad, it was released in May to coincide with the FA Cup Final, thus becoming the first ever domestic cup song and kickstarting the tradition that would also give us 'Blue is the Colour', 'Marching on Together' and FIVE different Chas & Dave songs.

The first — and probably best — of them, exactly one decade after Hill had shown the way (avoid being "too wordy" was Jimmy's sage advice), was 'Ossie's Dream'. While the shorthand title conjures a surreal dreamscape, the parenthetical long-form '(Spurs Are on Their Way to Wembley)' provides a candid description of one of the Argentinian midfielder's professional ambitions. In his autobiography, the title of which simulates the song, Ardiles wrote that it was "a 'true song', in the sense that I had always wanted to play at Wembley. It was, in a way, a mission of mine." This mission had been thwarted at the quarter-final stage in his previous two seasons as a Tottenham player, and then by national team manager César Luis Menotti declining to select European-based players for a friendly against England in May 1980, opting instead to bring over an experimental team of home-based youngsters that included the 19-year-old Diego Maradona.

Ossie's decade with Spurs was unhappily interrupted by the Falklands War, when international hostilities in a pre-globalised society made a season-long loan move across the Channel prudent, but his status as everyone's favourite Argentinian was largely untarnished by the conflict or by his compatriot's contentious 'hand of God' moment at the 1986 World Cup. The pintsize playmaker's enduring popularity owes a lot to his strength of character but also more than a little something to Chas & Dave. Case in point: Ricky Villa's slaloming run produced one of the greatest cup final goals of all time to win the trophy for Spurs, yet he is not as fondly remembered as Ossie. The Argentinian duo were both conferred with anglicised diminutives (Osvaldo became Ossie; Ricardo became Ricky) when they arrived at Tottenham in 1978 but only Ossie became mononymous in the same vein as Cher, Kylie and Adele. Granted, the uniqueness of a name plays a large part in that, but first-name terms tend to be reserved for national treasures, the kind of people that songs are written for or about. So, in a team containing home favourites Steve Perryman, Glenn Hoddle and Garth Crooks, what made Ossie special to the songwriters?

Certainly, in the days before the Premier League, the rarity of foreigners bestowed upon them a sense of intrigue and exoticism. Chas & Dave's homespun charm, however, is more pie, mash and Margate than picaña steak and Mar del Plata. In classic Del Boy fashion, the appeal of Ossie lay in his mangling of the foreign tongue, hence the unforgettable delivery of the line 'In de cup for Totting-ham'.

"That's how I said it, because that's how I thought you said it," Ardiles explains in his autobiography. "We never pronounce an 'h' in Spanish but in English, as far as I could tell, you did." Being a proficient linguist, he has long since corrected his pronunciation, although his teammates never let him forget about it. Another who had not forgotten was Dave's sister, Marie Brown, and it was a telephone conversation with her that provided inspiration. The original impetus for the record came from band manager Bob England who, like his charges, was a mad Tottenham fan and implored them to write a cup song as Spurs edged closer to Wembley while Chas & Dave were in the middle of a UK tour. As Dave Peacock explained the task at hand, his sister replied, "I've heard Ossie Ardiles on the wireless, he don't say 'Tottenham', he says 'Totting-ham'". And with that, Peacock had his hook.

The rest of the song was built around common chants. The opening gambit 'Ossie's going to Wembley/His knees have gone all trembly/ Come on you Spurs/Come on you Spurs' reworked the effervescent refrain from 'I Came, I Saw, I Conga'd', the Latin rhythms of which tend to evoke Brits abroad. It was in fact written by three white American men and its usage here popularised the 'We're on our way to Wembley' chant. Lyrical imagery came from the Shelf's battle cry of 'Keith's blue and white army'; 'Burkinshaw' rhyming with 'war' was the cue to weave Ossie's journey into a wider narrative of White Hart Lane soldiers marching on Wembley to capture the cup.

And Ossie needed the bravery of a soldier when he was marched into the intimidating terrain of Portland Studios. Inspiring the song was one thing but no one had told him about delivering the 'Tottenham' line solo. "I am by nature a rather shy and reserved man," he recounted. "I was like, 'No, no, no and no.'" A combination of peer pressure and being a good sport got the job done, and the Tottenham Hotspur FA Cup Final Squad Official Souvenir Record — as it was billed on the cover (Chas & Dave uncredited) — was hastily pressed and distributed. The wives of Chas Hodges and Bob England and a couple of other girls in Spurs kits personally delivered to north London record stores to get it in the charts the same week as the big match. It debuted at 45 but rose to number five when sales were boosted by a replay and eventual Spurs victory.

The B-side to 'Ossie's Dream' is perhaps even more renowned but is not an original Tottenham song. Like 'When the Saints Go Marching In', 'Glory, Glory, [insert name with matching number of syllables]' has multiple claims on it. Like 'Saints', it also began life on the opposite side of the Atlantic, as an American Civil War song. 'The Battle Hymn of the Republic' was composed by abolitionist Julia Ward Howe and became known as 'Glory, Glory, Hallelujah' outside of the States. Tottenham brought it to the English game in the early-Sixties, apparently first singing it in April 1960 when a 3-1 win at Molineux scuppered Wolverhampton Wanderers' hopes of securing the league and cup double that Spurs themselves would achieve the following season. And it was during the European Cup adventures of 1961-62 that it assumed anthem status. Following a first-round tie against Górnik Zabrze, the Polish press referred to a tough-tackling Spurs team, beaten 4-2, as “no angels”. In the return leg at White Hart Lane, the supporters’ coordinated response was to don wings and halos and daub placards with “Rejoice! This is the night of vengeance”. ‘Glory, Glory, Tottenham Hotspur’ was heartily sung during an 8-1 victory (10-5 on aggregate) and it has been an exalted part of their repertoire ever since.

In 1967, it was recorded by the FA Cup-winning team, bookending medleys that also contained ‘Hello Dolly’, ‘I Was Kaiser Bill’s Batman’ and ‘It’s a Grand Old Team’ as part of *The Spurs Go Marching On EP: Glory Glory Hallelujah, etc.* ‘Glory Glory Leeds United’ by Ronnie Hilton followed a year later in celebration of their twin glories in the League Cup and Inter-Cities Fairs Cup. Manchester United were relative latecomers, releasing ‘Glory Glory Man United’ as a 1983 FA Cup Final single, abetted by Frank Renshaw, rhythm guitarist and backing vocalist for Manchester’s answer to the Beatles, Herman’s Hermits. The three English giants were beaten, however, by Hibernian. In the late-Fifties, Hector Nicol with the Kelvin Country Dance Band issued a double A-side of ‘Glory, Glory to the Hi-bees (Hibernian Supporters’ Song)’ and ‘The Boys in Maroon (Song to the ‘Hearts of Mid-Lothian’)’, which is akin to ‘Glory, Glory, Tottenham Hotspur’ being paired with ‘Good Old Arsenal’! Like an adulterous Chas & Dave, Scottish comedian Nicol hawked himself to the whole of Dundee as well as Edinburgh; he also wrote and sang ‘Dark Blue of Dundee’ and ‘The Terrors of Tannadice’, despite being a St Mirren supporter deep down.

By contrast, Chas & Dave doubled down on their Hotspur love by releasing ‘Tottenham, Tottenham’ when the Lilywhites made it back to Wembley for the 1982 FA Cup Final. The inspiration this time came from Chubby Checker, with the lyrical theme of ‘We’re gonna do it like we did last year’ bootlegged from the rock ’n’ roller’s ‘Let’s twist again, like we did last summer’. Ossie got another namecheck

('Like when Ossie's dream came true') and Spurs again won after a replay, but despite being readied more than a week in advance, 'Tottenham, Tottenham' couldn't quite recapture the magic of 'Ossie's Dream', peaking at 19 in the charts.

'Hot Shot Tottenham!' (1987), went one better but its ascent up the charts was impeded by a nerve-shredding 3-2 defeat to Coventry City, best remembered for Keith Houchen's flying header and Gary Mabbutt's luckless own goal in extra time. Not forgetting Ossie, which the lyrics predictably didn't, the Argentinian was subbed off for defender Gary Stevens at the end of 90 minutes. Following Mabbutt's slice of misfortune, Belgian forward Nico Claesen was thrown into the mix but failed to make a mark. Similarly, Peacock recalls trying to get Claesen to imitate Ossie's infamous pronunciation but 'he couldn't get his tongue around it'. 'Hot Shot Tottenham!' had a second lease of life in 2015 when tribute act Ledley and the Kings updated 'David Pleat's blue and white army' to 'Pochettino's...' to mark a run to the League Cup Final.

When Gazza arrowed a 30-yard free kick past David Seaman in the first ever FA Cup semi-final to be played at Wembley, Chas & Dave had a field day. 'When the Year Ends in One' took listeners on a potted history of Tottenham Hotspur honours and cemented the superstition that trophies followed a new decade, as they had in 1901, 1921, 1951, 1961, 1971, 1981 and would again in 1991 when Nottingham Forest were subsequently vanquished. This lucky omen evidently only applied to the 20th century. 'When the Year Ends in One' was backed by a reprise of 'Ossie's Dream' but still couldn't break the top 40. 'The Victory Song (We're Off to Wembley 'Cos We Beat the Arsenal)' was a bonus release, big on bragging rights, but which also failed to bother the charts. Nevertheless, Chas & Dave now had enough material for their own Tottenham compilation album and their songs remain jukebox favourites. Jimmy Hill told *The Guardian* in 2005 that he was still earning about £57.20 in annual royalties, but no one's still singing 'Good Old Arsenal' in north London pubs.

Reviews

"I must say I didn't like it when we were doing it, I didn't like it when it was released, and I didn't like it after that either. Now I've come to appreciate it more. My most serious concern remained the football, however. I felt the spotlight on me: my knees were trembling as the day [of the final] approached and suddenly 'the road to Wembley' wasn't so much a jingle or a joke recording, more like my biggest footballing dream."

– our eponymous hero Ossie Ardiles

"It's the quickest song I ever wrote. I wrote it in about two minutes."

– Dave Peacock, interviewed by *The Morning Star* in 2021

"It was at this point that the football song took its first steps to respectability. Because even though 'Ossie's Dream' ticked all the traditional boxes — namely a terrace-friendly tune and self-aggrandising lyrics — the addition of a sense of humour and a dose of lyrical self-awareness moved the goalposts entirely."

– Robert Collins, 'The Life and Death of the English Football Song', *Pop Matters* (2008)

"I've actually written a football tune and I'm really hoping Spurs might be interested. Ideally it's a song for the FA Cup Final, when the time comes. I love all the old Spurs singles by Chas & Dave, they're real classics."

– Supergrass drummer and Tottenham fan Danny Goffey, speaking in 2008 about an unrealised ambition

11. Come On You Reds

First released: 1994
Highest UK chart position: 1

If Tottenham were the most prolific soccer-music crossover act of the Eighties, then the Nineties belonged to Manchester United. The obvious reason for this is the eleven major trophies they amassed throughout the decade. As the Nineties got under way, however, no one outside of Manchester was paying very much attention to Tracey Malone's 'It's Man. United (I'm So Excited)' or her melodic boast, to the tune of the Pointer Sisters, that they had 'Fergie, Incey, Les Sealey, he's the best'!

United fans had had little to cheer since the days of their 'Belfast Boy' George Best, and their aural highpoint predated even that most rock 'n' roll of footballers. In the summer of 1957, Trinidadian crooner Edric Connor's 'Manchester United Calypso' immortalised the Busby Babes on vinyl, mere months before the Munich air disaster would rob Old Trafford of eight of the players serenaded in the song, as well as the swagger that both they and Connor emitted. The mass appeal of Duncan Edwards et al. is perhaps best summed up by the Salford-born poet of punk John Cooper Clarke waxing lyrical in his memoir about the 'glamorous, world-class club ... with a bestselling calypso record dedicated to them'.

'Manchester United Calypso' was in part a riposte to Edmundo Ros's 'Exotic Football Calypso of 1953', which attempted to settle a pub debate on the best teams in England, with Manchester United (1951-52 champions) omitted from a list that included Arsenal, Newcastle United, Tottenham Hotspur, Blackpool, West Bromwich Albion and Portsmouth. Lord Kitchener with Fitzroy Coleman's Band beat Edric Connor to the punch by releasing 'The Manchester Football Double' in 1956, which started promisingly by stating 'Football and footballers / at Manchester / you find the headquarters' but, as the title suggests, its inclusion of United and City meant that it was embraced by neither. Indeed, the terrace version of Connor's calypso contains an unofficial verse denigrating the Sky Blues.

Despite being a trailblazer as one of the first black people to make inroads at the BBC, it would be fallacious to credit 'Manchester United Calypso' solely to Connor. It was actually written by 16-year-old Eric Watterson for a newspaper competition and arranged by Ken Jones, who was a collaborator with psychedelic-rock band the Zombies and worked regularly in film and TV. Astonishingly, football calypso encompasses so many acts that it merits an idiosyncratic sub-genre of its own; as well as the aforementioned 'Norwich City Calypso', Johnny Cobnut stoked East Anglia's Tractor Derby with the opposing 'Ipswich Football Calypso', and Ronnie Hilton (rivalling Chas & Dave for fecundity) produced the 'Leeds United Calypso'.

Laidback Caribbean grooves were not in the air when Manchester United went to Wembley in 1990. In the third-round tie against Nottingham Forest, the atmosphere had been mutinous and Mark Robins' winning goal that day is widely credited with saving Alex Ferguson's job and setting him on the way to becoming the most decorated manager in the English game (and a sir to boot). It still took a replay to see off the unfancied Crystal Palace, who were 'Glad

All Over' just to reach the final and celebrated by releasing their own version of the fan anthem, which has been riotously sung at Selhurst Park ever since hitmakers the Dave Clark Five played there in 1968. Its positive vibes were supplemented by soaring B-side 'Where Eagles Fly'. Manchester United's cup final single, by contrast, was the staid 'We Will Stand Together', backed by 'We Will Stand Together Again', emphasis on unity (and repetition) rather than exuberance.

The tempo increased as the Nineties progressed and the players found their groove. Madonna-in-a-shell-suit Tracey Malone soundtracked the road to Rotterdam, where they beat Barcelona to lift the European Cup Winners' Cup the following year. By 1993, the fans were back on side and 'United (We Love You)', released to celebrate winning the inaugural Premier League (the club's first championship trophy since topping the Second Division in 1975), scraped into the top 40. Like Liverpool in 1963, Manchester United were on the cusp of something special, with football and pop culture converging to crystallise the moment.

Now, not even the most myopic United supporter could make a case for their heavily derided 'anthem' matching the cultural significance of 'You'll Never Walk Alone', but each song tells its own story and 'Come On You Reds' landed just as the Cool Britannia facsimile of the Swinging Sixties was coalescing, with the laddish attitudes of *Loaded* and Oasis pushing football and Manchester to the forefront of pop culture. Into this social maelstrom strode Eric Cantona, Ryan Giggs and ... er, Status Quo.

Taking its lead from the nascent Premier League, the pairing of Manchester United with Status Quo, two veritable institutions, owed more to commercial opportunism than anything else. Quo frontmen Francis Rossi and Rick Parfitt were both Tottenham fans but, with Chas & Dave already occupying the role of resident Spurs songsmiths, they did what so many other Cockney Reds have done and looked north in search of glory, no doubt encouraged by record label Polygram and a run of underwhelming chart positions broken only by 'The Anniversary Waltz', which traded on past glories in much the same way that Manchester United had for the previous three decades. The last time that the Red Devils had been the dominant force in English football, the Quo were still known as the Spectres, but their trad-rock longevity meant that they formed a sentimental bridge between eras and were thus welcomed to Old Trafford in a way that fashionable London upstarts such as Blur or Suede probably never would have been.

Status Quo's detractors accuse them of recycling the same simple twelve-bar blues, but sniping at a half-century career containing more than 60 chart hits is a bit like telling Fergie he got the formation wrong as he lifts his umpteenth Premier League trophy. The same colour-by-numbers approach was applied to writing a football anthem — wallowing in past glories: check ... a rapid run-through of the current team roster: check ... fist-pumping platitudes: check — and it resulted in the only club-issued football single to ever reach number one in the UK charts. For a fortnight, Manchester United could claim the unique treble of being league champions, FA Cup holders and top of the pops!

Living up to their name, which suggests more of the same, the song was a rewrite of Status Quo's number five hit from 1988, 'Burning Bridges (On and Off and On Again)'. And here's that lyrical checklist:

- Sentimentality — the opening line 'Busby Babes they always make me cry' is an alliterative substitute for (and negation of) 'Burning bridges never made me cry';
- Smells like team spirit — 'Schmeichel, Parker, Pallister / Irwin, Bruce, Sharpe and Ince / Hughes, McClair, Keane and Cantona / Robson, Kanchelskis and Giggs'. Pity poor Clayton Blackmore and Mike Phelan who had to sing along in honour of their teammates without getting a mention themselves;
- Rabble-rousing gestures — a quick burst of 'Glory glory Man United' ensures that a small part of the song translates to the terraces, even if it is a direct steal from those it seeks to inspire.

Whatever its merits, 'Come On You Reds' represents a late-career highpoint for Status Quo, who have not returned to the top ten since. By the time Euro '96 came around, they were locked in a court battle with BBC Radio 1 to determine whether the station's playlists should be the preserve of youthful cool or whatever's selling well; the Quo lost and were relegated to the same league as Mr Blobby, Robson and Jerome, and Cliff Richard.

For Manchester United, the song represented another step towards world domination. The imposing presence of Peter Schmeichel in United's #1 shirt also propelled it to the top of the charts in Denmark, and a jaunty Irish jig element made it a bestseller with the nearest overseas fanbase on the Emerald Isle. Quite what Roy Keane thought of Lee Sharpe's air guitar has never been placed on record, but one of the intimidating Irishman's trademark glowers would probably suffice. It's equally easy to imagine Sir Alex Ferguson disapproving of his team playing pop stars, as evidenced by the friction David Beckham's celebrity lifestyle with Posh Spice generated. The manager is a notable absentee from all of United's musical escapades. However, in spite of his iron fist, Ferguson was an astute empire builder who understood the economics of the Premier League and recognised the importance of marketing exercises, even if they weren't necessarily to his taste.

Ferguson also possessed a talent for reinvention. If 'Come On You Reds' was a last hurrah for Status Quo, then the same could be said for two of the goalscorers in the 1994 FA Cup Final; with the 'Class of '92' waiting in the wings, the careers of Mark Hughes and Brian McClair were being wound down. Ferguson's ability to change a winning formula and sprinkle stardust on grim surroundings could be considered Bowie-esque, although the cantankerous demeanours and overseeing of occasionally rancorous line-up changes probably makes the Fall's Mark E. Smith a more fitting comparison.

Though Manchester United would go on to scale greater footballing heights, 'Come On You Reds' marks a musical zenith, in commercial terms at least. 1995's 'We're Gonna Do It Again', featuring the rapper Stryker, was wholly inaccurate, stalling at six in the charts and presaging cup final defeat to Everton. The following year, United were again victorious at Wembley but 'Move Move Move (The Red Tribe)' was outdone in the charts by 'Pass and Move (It's the Liverpool Groove)', both of which resembled a bunch of chavs channelling Reel 2 Real and the Mad Stuntman. Finally, the swooping guitars of 'Lift it High (All About Belief)' perhaps should have marked a new highpoint, especially as it commemorated the treble of 1999. The *NME*'s James Oldham even described it, without sarcasm, as "heartfelt, soaring and beautiful". Belief undoubtedly played a part in the incredible late show against Bayern Munich, but that historic victory wasn't all about Solskjær and Sheringham's state of mind. And belief definitely doesn't convert to record sales, or there'd be far more successful *X Factor* contestants. Just as on-pitch success is an amalgam of many factors, there is a mysterious alchemy involved in determining winners and losers in the music business.

Reviews

"I've had more number one singles than Noel Gallagher has had as a solo artist and I can't even sing."

– Gary Neville stoking inner-city rivalries in *The Athletic*, June 2023

"It's amazing how the sound engineers can make you sound. The technology was good, even then. People took weeks to record shit, we did it in an afternoon ... We had a few cans to help the vocal cords, but it wasn't a massive session."

– Brian McClair, also quoted in *The Athletic*

"Only Lee Sharpe and Brian McClair, sporting some gruff rock star stubble for the occasion, appeared to be enjoying themselves. Brandishing unplugged guitars they played the role of pop stars with an appetite that suggests both would have enjoyed the real thing. Sharpe, as we know, was pretty much living the lifestyle already. But not even he could appear cool singing along to these lyrics."

– Will Tidey, *Life With Sir Alex: A Fan's Story of Ferguson's 25 Years at Manchester United*

"[Compared to other football songs] 'Come On You Reds' was Bacharach and David — and certainly it's crafted enough to have all the elements you'd want in a Cup Final song. Only a decision to marinade the song in trebly, plastic keyboards spoils the mood. It's still terrible, but it's the right kind of terrible, just about."

– popular-number1s.com

"I bought NTL [the Quo's 14th album *Never Too Late*, released 1981] when it came out and had heard most of the albums by then. Couldn't tell you what order I heard them all. I continued to buy everything they did until they did 'Come On You Reds!'"

– loyal fan 'rossiswaistcoat' has their say on the Status Quo Fan Forum

12. El Cant del Barça

First released: 1974
Highest UK chart position: N/A

"*Més que un club.*" It's inkeeping with FC Barcelona's pious self-image as the Church of Catalonia that their anthems are alternatively described as hymns, even as the club's holier-than-thou identity is at risk of being sacrificed on the altar of 21st-century commercialism.

'*El Cant del Barça*' is the latest in a line of 'hymns' stretching back a century. While most British anthems are appropriated pop songs or quickly cobbled-together paeans to cup glory, Barcelona emulate Norwich in preferring specially-commissioned concertos, although, as we've learnt, even 'On the Ball, City' was semi-appropriated. The first such canticle, '*Himno del FC Barcelona*', unveiled in February 1923, was composed by Enric Morera with lyrics by poet and linguist Rafael Folch i Capdevila. It was premiered at the recently opened Camp de Les Corts, Barcelona's home between 1922 and 1957, by Orfeó Gracienc, a choral society that has since been honoured for its preservation of the Catalan identity. Catalan nationalism provides a thematic chain linking the hymns to the football club, each being written in the Catalan language and with the original grandiloquent lyrics of Capdevila emphasising the relationship between '*esport i pàtria*' (sport and homeland). This archetypal hymn was composed in tribute to Joan Gamper, a larger-than-life figurehead for Catalonia who was actually born Hans Max Gamper-Haessig in Switzerland, in 1877.

Gamper was a keen sportsman and prosperous businessman who had already founded FC Zürich when, in 1899, he stopped off in Barcelona to visit an uncle while on his way to Africa to establish a sugar trading company. He fell in love with the city and instead of an export business, he instead founded a football club that he envisaged as being open to everyone, regardless of their background, and democratically governed by its members. Initially concentrating on playing, Gamper (now known by the Catalan version of his name, Joan, which dropped the German Hs that the native tongue struggled with) was the first captain of FC Barcelona and a prolific striker, netting 126 goals in just 55 matches. He would later serve as club president on five separate occasions between 1908 and 1925 and was instrumental in moving them into their own stadium at Les Corts. The growing success of Les Corts and its football team would, however, also be the source of its founder's tragic downfall.

In June 1925, before a post-season friendly against CE Júpiter, the British Royal Marine band (then anchored in the port of Barcelona) took to the field to perform the Spanish national anthem, which was loudly jeered by proud Catalans, who then applauded 'God Save the King'. The Primo de Rivera dictatorship accused Gamper of promoting Catalan nationalism, punishing him with expulsion from Spain and the closure of Les Corts for the next six months. In July 1930, beset by personal and financial difficulties, Gamper committed suicide. His funeral was thronged with public well-wishers and Barcelona players carried the coffin to its final resting place in the Montjuïc Cemetery.

The hymn to Gamper perhaps should have stood the test of time, but its wider circulation was hamstrung by both the forced closure of Les Corts and its coming before the age of commercial sound recording technology. A second hymn was commissioned in 1949, on the occasion of FC Barcelona's 50th anniversary. '*Barcelona, semper amunt!*' (Barcelona, always up!) possessed the same imperial choral tones, its score composed by Joan Dotras. The bravery of lyricist Esteve Calzada was in not departing from what had gone before; it was written in Catalan despite the oppressive Franco regime banning the language from public events. Unsurprisingly under such circumstances, '*Barcelona, semper amunt!*' also found itself suppressed.

By the time of the third hymn in 1957, Franco was still in charge, but his autocratic governance was being diluted by a boom in industry and tourism that made the region one of Europe's largest metropolitan areas. And proclaiming boom time was the construction of Camp Nou, literally meaning 'new field', increasing spectator capacity from the relatively modest 60,000 of Camp de Les Corts to a whopping 90,000. There are unsubstantiated claims that Camp Nou was to be named after Joan Gamper but that any such plans were overruled by the Franco dictatorship, which didn't take kindly to such a prominent monument bearing the name of a liberal foreigner who had committed suicide — still deemed sinful in Catholic Spain.

The stadium's inauguration took place on 24 September 1957, coinciding with the annual festival of La Mercè, the patron saint of Barcelona. The first half of the opening ceremony was presided over by the Archbishop of Barcelona and included a solemn mass and a commanding rendition of 'Hallelujah' from Handel's *Messiah*. It was attended by Franco dignitaries and approximately 45,000 spectators. The stands were packed for the more celebratory second part, which included dances and a club parade. To the strains of '*Himne a l'Estadi*' (Hymn to the Stadium) by Josep Badia and Adolf Cabané, 11,000 white doves were released into the stadium. Again written in Catalan, '*Himne a l'Estadi*' is best remembered for being the first time that the then lesser-used diminutive 'Barça' was expressed in music.

'*Himne a l'Estadi*' was still receiving airplay in 1974 when '*El Cant del Barça*' entered the canon. Celebrating the club's diamond jubilee, composer Manuel Valls i Gorinha was the winner of a public contest. Jaume Picas and Josep Maria Espinàs were tasked with writing accompanying lyrics and could have been taking notes from 'Blue is the Colour', released two years beforehand. Though they refrain from stating 'blaugrana is the colour', the lyrics translate as follows:

> Blue and scarlet in the wind,
> Our cry is bold,
> We have a name
> That everyone knows:
> Barça, Barça, Barça.

It is a hymn to the colour of the club and its supporters. Its premiere was as pompous as its predecessors; led by conductor Oriol Martorell, a 3,600-strong choir belted it out in a pre-match ceremony. However, the upbeat melody and handclap interludes made it more convivial and audience-friendly than the hymns that had gone before. It also received a vinyl release, the Coral Sant Jordi performance becoming the definitive version.

Though already popular with supporters, its status as the definitive Barça anthem was sealed by another controversial club president by the name of Joan. During his first tenure, beginning in 2003, Joan Laporta added to the pre-match rituals by demanding that the Nou Camp's big screens be turned into a giant karaoke machine displaying the words of '*El Cant del Barça*' for everyone to sing along to. This contrived attempt at generating atmosphere might not have been popular with the *Boixos Nois* ultras, who allegedly schemed to kidnap the 'Catalan Kennedy', but two decades on it's become a tradition. The song has also transcended its Catalan roots; no doubt with an eye on the global market, it has been translated into the language of every player to have worn the famous blaugrana jersey, with the different iterations available for your listening pleasure at the FC Barcelona Museum.

A further hymn, '*Cant del Centenari*' (Hymn of the Centenary), was commissioned for the club's hundredth-birthday celebrations, but its clanging cymbals and sober descant provided no serious competition to the anthemic credentials of '*El Cant del Barça*'. Greater competition comes, not unexpectedly, from the other half of *El Clásico*.

Real Madrid lacked a bespoke anthem to rival '*El Cant* ... ' until '*¡Hala Madrid! ... y nada más*' was commissioned by club president Florentino Pérez to commemorate *La Décima*, Madrid's 10th European Cup / Champions League in 2014. Somewhat late to the party, Madrid nevertheless bucked the 21st-century decline in recorded football anthems, powering to number one in the Spanish charts just as Manchester United had done in the UK 20 years before. '*¡Hala Madrid! ... y nada más*' (Go Madrid ... and nothing more) has overall fared better than 'Come On You Reds', however. It regularly emanates from the stands of the Santiago Bernabéu Stadium and a short burst of the track is deployed for goal celebrations.

For all their dissension, the similarities between Spain's two superpowers are uncanny. Just as at Barcelona, there had been earlier anthems which failed to impress. The plain '¡Hala Madrid!' was commissioned by Real Madrid's version of Joan Gamper, former forward and president Santiago Bernabéu de Yeste, and recorded by José de Aguilar in 1952. And in 2002, '*Himno del centenario*' was recorded by the internationally acclaimed tenor Plácido Domingo but failed to gain any wider plaudits. Domingo also covered '*¡Hala Madrid! ... y nada más*' for release in 2016 after the less-celebrated *la undécima*.

The original was the brainchild of Nadir Khayat, a Moroccan-Swedish producer who performs and records under the alias RedOne. The desire to abandon Lady Gaga, Nicki Minaj and Pitbull for something "more classic and symphonic" yet also chantable had been brewing for a few years. *El Mundo* journalist Manuel Jabois was enlisted to provide the words, which appealed to the egotistical Pérez by appealing to Real's record-breaking history and galácticos philosophy ('The stars are now coming out / My old Chamartín / From far away and from nearby / You gather us all here').

There's a fine line between confidence and presumption, and Ronaldo, Ramos, Bale, Benzema, Modrić, Marcelo, Ancelotti and the rest had recorded the song well in advance of the May showdown with Atlético Madrid. With *La Décima* secured by a 4-1 victory against their nearest geographical rivals, it was released to the public the very next day and charted in Sweden, Hungary, Costa Rica, Israel, Mexico and Slovakia, as well as Spain.

In the new world order dictated by Florentino Pérez rather than General Franco, the more humble and sacrosanct customs of Catalonia meant FC Barcelona were in danger of being left behind. Gamper's founding vision of a club with a strong social conscience and community identity had become so entrenched that they eschewed shirt sponsorship until 2006. Having paradoxically profited reputationally from not being besmirched by corporate logos, even when the iconic kit did yield to having an insignia across the chest it was still very much counter to the money-driven normality of the modern game, instead gifting premium advertising space to the international children's charity UNICEF. Laporta announced at an executive committee meeting, "through Unicef, we, the people of FC Barcelona, the people of 'Barça', are very proud to donate our shirt to the children of the world who are our present, but especially are our future".

Fast-forward 16 years to his second tenure as president and he's singing from a slightly different hymn sheet. Facing debts rumoured to total €1.35 billion, Barcelona joined forces with the Swedish audio streaming platform Spotify in a "strategic relationship through which we seek to bring together two worlds that can arouse emotion, namely music and football" (c/o Juli Guiu, Marketing VP). Selling naming rights to Spotify Camp Nou aroused some emotion among the puritans, although as with St James' temporary rebrand as the Sports Direct Arena, nobody outside of marketing circles will ever refer to it as such. The Spotify revolution, which allows users to access pretty much every song ever written from their smartphone or any handy internet-enabled device, was always technological as opposed to musical; while content creators rage against the streaming royalty rate, the business creator, Daniel Ek, has become immeasurably wealthier than any musician who's ever lived.

Besides lucrative sponsorship deals, fruits of the strategic relationship have included a limited-edition shirt emblazoned with the October's Very Own owl logo to celebrate Canadian rapper Drake, who owns the OVO brand, being the first artist to reach 50 billion Spotify streams, and the addition of Catalan as the 63rd language the platform became available in, several months after the alliance was announced in early 2022. On the latter development, Laporta commented: "They have understood our culture from the outset, and their commitment to Catalan, the club's official language, through the development of the Spotify app in our language is testament to precisely that."

According to Tim Crow, a sports sponsorship advisor, it is more testament to Spotify looking to win over their new customer base. "Spotify will have to work very hard to earn the respect of Barça fans. Just because they write a big cheque, ride into town and their brand is everywhere doesn't mean Barca fans will welcome them," he told SportsPro Media. Summing up the relationship, Crow opined: "You've got two brands who are both looking for new meaning in a changed world".

A statement of the club's brand identity is hiding in plain sight among Spotify's never-ending catalogue of songs, but perhaps the ageing '*El Cant del Barça*' is crying out for a remix.

Reviews

"The writers were talking about Barça as a club of social integration ... It's a song for all the fans. You identify with it. It refers to the union between players and fans. It's about tradition, the goals we've celebrated together. You feel you're part of a group, part of a family."

– Carles Santacana Torres, Professor of Contemporary History at the University of Barcelona

"*Totes unides fem força.*"

– the title of the first part of Aitana Bonmatí's biography is the feminine version of the line 'Tots units fem força' (United we are strong); Bonmatí came through Barça's La Masia academy and was the recipient of the Golden Ball for player of the tournament when Spain won the 2023 Women's World Cup

"Xavi's wife Nuria Cunillera has posted an adorable video on Instagram today, which shows her husband teaching their son Dan how to sing '*Cant del Barça*'."

– the Barcelona manager engages in the same indoctrination as the average football fan according to *Football España* (31/01/23)

Club Anthems Spotify Chart

As per 18 December 2022, the day former Barcelona golden boy Lionel Messi lifted the World Cup.

#	Song	Streams
1	You'll Never Walk Alone *Gerry and the Pacemakers*	77,885,545
2	Blue Moon *The Marcels*	35,209,439
3	When the Saints Go Marching In *Louis Armstrong*	6,507,550
4	El Cant del Barça *Coral Sant Jordi (Official Version)*	3,334,463
5	Leeds! Leeds! Leeds! (Marching on Together) *Leeds United Team & Supporters*	2,136,510
6	Blue is the Colour *Chelsea Football Club*	1,958,484
7	I'm Forever Blowing Bubbles *Cockney Rejects*	1,396,773
8	Theme from Z-Cars *Johnny Keating and the Z-Men*	664,609
9	Ossie's Dream (Spurs Are on Their Way to Wembley) *Tottenham Hotspur FA Cup Final Squad*	568,307
10	The Blaydon Races *The Fans (N.U.F.C.)*	345,629
11	Come On You Reds *International Sports United* *	95,277
12	On the Ball, City *1959 Version*	18,468

*The Manchester United Football Squad version is unavailable. Like Chas & Dave, Status Quo were never officially credited. Does the missing sound recording suggest remorse on the part of whoever owns the copyright?

Side B: International Hits

1. El Rock del Mundial

First released: 1962
Highest UK chart position: N/A

Between the Broadway debut of 'You'll Never Walk Alone' and its terrace adoption and the Merseybeat invasion of North America, Los Ramblers of Chile taught the football world how to rock.

On 22 May 1960, two years before Los Ramblers found fame, Chile had, literally, rocked. The Valdivia earthquake, measuring 9.5 on the moment magnitude scale, remains the most powerful tremor ever recorded, causing tsunamis that battered the Chilean coast and sent waves as high as 35ft travelling 10,000km across the Pacific Ocean. Death toll estimates range from 1,000 to 6,000 and communities throughout the country were devastated. In such a mortal context, organising and hosting a World Cup became a titanic challenge, but also a welcome tonic.

Chile had registered its candidacy for the 1962 World Cup in 1954, with South America the guaranteed destination after their federations had threatened to boycott if a third consecutive tournament were awarded to a European nation. Argentina, strong favourites off the back of previous bids, were the main competition. At a FIFA Congress meeting in 1956, Argentinian spokesperson Raul Colombo declared: "*Podemos hacer el Mundial mañana mismo. Lo tenemos todo* — We can start the World Cup tomorrow. We have it all." By contrast, Chile targeted the FIFA statute outlining the tournament's role in supporting less developed countries, with Carlos Dittborn Pinto, head of the Chilean committee, arguing "*Porque nada tenemos, lo haremos todo* — Because we have nothing, we will do everything."

Chile won by 32 votes to 11 and Dittborn's words became the tournament's slogan, made even more profound by the events of May 1960. Dittborn himself would not live to see the tournament he fought so hard to secure and sustain. In April 1962, one month before the competition's start, he suffered a fatal heart attack aged only 38. It is generally thought that the burden of organising an international festival against a backdrop of natural disasters and hardship was a contributing factor to his untimely death. The country mourned the man who had brought them the World Cup, with a tribute in magazine *Vea* stating: "It is wrong to attribute his achievement to a few nicely turned words — it was actually thanks to his overwhelming enthusiasm, his limitless tenacity and his contagious optimism."

The same accolade could be applied to Jorge Rojas Astorga, the bandleader of Los Ramblers. Rojas was a prodigious musician whose talent at the piano was self-taught. However, despite coming from a nurturing musical home, music didn't represent a practical career choice. Instead, Rojas followed the family printing trade while also pursuing his first-choice vocation with the formation of his own orchestra. The eight-piece Los Ramblers was born in 1959 and quickly found favour with Don Ricardo Garcia, one of Chile's leading disc jockeys, who invited them to play on his weekly '*Show de la polla*' (Show of the Cock). They had a certain strut but, like the early Rolling Stones, the embryonic Ramblers were essentially a covers act and their own revolving door of members began turning long before Brian Jones fatally mixed narcotics with swimming.

As the 1962 World Cup hove into view, Rojas turned his attention to profiteering. Commercial exploits were popping up everywhere and his first idea was hats. "I had a printing press with my father, and since the '62 World Cup was going to attract a lot of people, I suggested that we sell hats for the sun. But we had zero experience," Rojas recalled. "Everyone managed to make money with the event that had all of Chile excited. People put pastry shops around the national stadium. Then I thought: if I have a band, I'd better make a World Cup song."

Full marks for originality, because no previous showpiece had come with its own song. Rojas began writing towards the end of 1961 and '*El Rock del Mundial*' (The Rock of the World) came quickly, the music composed in one day and the lyrics written in three, although it was nearly quite different. It was going to begin with a brassy sax solo but the saxophonist hired for the premiere performance was a no-show, apparently having fallen asleep, so former band member Oscar Soto claims to have reinvented the introduction as a catchy guitar riff in a matter of minutes. Furthermore, the lyrics originally namechecked left-winger Leonel Sánchez and right-winger Jaime Ramírez, who had both attended the same Santiago primary school as Rojas. Pleased to have honoured his contemporaries, especially as trying to fit Ramírez to the tune had delayed the song's completion, Rojas was persuaded by his godfather to remove them with an eye on longevity: if it became a hit, names would date it, went his warden's argument.

The song debuted at a corporate Christmas event and was so well received that enthusiastic attendees requested it be played twice more. Noting the reaction of revellers, the manager of the Casino de Viña offered the band a residency, which in turn brought them to the attention of Camilo Fernández, artistic director of the RCA label and on the lookout for an act to launch his own Demon imprint. Los Ramblers entered the recording studio in late March 1962 and two months later, on the eve of the World Cup, '*El Rock del Mundial*' was released.

It was an immediate hit, and only grew in popularity as the host nation progressed. Chile won their opening match 3-1 against Switzerland in front of a crowd of more than 65,000, with the deleted Sánchez and Ramírez responsible for all three goals. Ramírez scored again in the next match, a 2-0 win against Italy, which put to the test the air of conviviality generated by '*El Rock del Mundial*'.

The antagonistic tone to a match that became known as the Battle of Santiago was instead set by Italian journalists who, entirely unappreciative of the adversity that Dittborn and his organising committee had overcome, described their hosts as prone to "malnutrition, illiteracy, alcoholism and poverty". In a coruscating article, Antonio Ghirelli and Corrado Pizzinelli summed up Chile thus: "This country and its people are proudly miserable and backwards." Understandably, the Chilean press hit back, stereotyping the Italians as fascist drug runners and forcing the offending scribes to flee the country.

The open hostilities continued on the pitch. The first foul was committed within 12 seconds. Italian midfielder Giorgio Ferrini was sent off in the eighth minute for a scathing challenge, but refused to leave the pitch and the local police intervened for the first of four times, dragging him off. Sánchez escaped being sent off for a retaliatory left hook on Italian right-back Mario David; in the ensuing melee another Sánchez left hook broke Humberto Maschio's nose but he still wasn't given his marching orders by English referee Ken Aston, who would later be inspired to invent red and yellow cards. When highlights reached British shores, they were infamously introduced by BBC commentator David Coleman as "the most stupid, appalling, disgusting and disgraceful exhibition of football, possibly in the history of the game".

The knockout stages were tame by comparison, although a relatively routine quarter-final victory over the Soviet Union foreshadowed a darker, yet less competitive encounter between the same nations in a qualifying play-off for the 1974 World Cup, a fixture Chile won by walkover because their opponents objected to playing at the Estadio Nacional de Chile, where enemies of the newly installed Pinochet regime had been executed two months previously. In the more festive and patriotic climate of 1962, the cries were only of '*ceacheí*'.

By this point, Los Ramblers had embarked on a nationwide tour and the call-response chant which lies at the heart of Rojas's auxiliary national anthem could be heard everywhere. *Ceacheí* alludes to the initial letters of Chile (CHI) but the cry of encouragement was not the composer's own invention. It is believed to have first been heard at the 1927 South American Athletics Championships and was first written into the lyrics of '*Romántico viajero*' (Romantic Traveller), the anthem of the Universidad de Chile soccer club, composed by Julio Cordero Vallejos in 1933. Rojas's masterstroke was setting the communal call to the burgeoning international language of rock 'n' roll, accented with hand claps and refs' whistles.

Though Chile stumbled at the semi-final stage, losing 4-2 to eventual champions Brazil, a thriving national team and the modern sound of '*El Rock del Mundial*' had combined to bring pride to their people. Los Ramblers became pioneers of the Chilean new wave by proving that ambitious local acts could bring their own Spanish inflections to pop music rather than being pale imitations of American rock 'n' rollers.

Claiming third place with a last-minute goal against Yugoslavia remains the pinnacle of Chile's World Cup achievements, and Los Ramblers have never bettered '*El Rock del Mundial*'. Doing so would be quite some feat since it is the best-selling single in Chilean musical history. Official sales figures are disputed: Rojas estimates 800,000 in the first two weeks, Fernández claims only 600,000 up to the end of the century, whereas a newspaper in 1999 reported sales approaching ten million. One reason given for suppressed sales is that the label lacked the infrastructure to press and ship such large quantities. Another explanation for discrepancies is that Fernández kept sales undisclosed to avoid taxation, giving rise to fantasy figures from some parties.

Suspect accounting, musical differences and personality clashes, particularly between Rojas and vacillating lead singer Germán Casas, make Los Ramblers' history read a little like the match reports from Chile versus Italy, yet they were still touring in celebration of the golden anniversary of '*El Rock*' in 2012. As so often happens, time, place and music magically coalesced, although watching the popular YouTube video that sets the song to footage of the third-place play-off, featuring the most socially awkward pitch invasion ever witnessed, shows that not quite everyone was hip to the groove in '62 ...

Reviews

"I remember that when Chile beat the Soviet Union, we were in Antofagasta and we had to play the song about 10 times!"

– sometime lead singer Germán Casas

"It is classic rock and roll, with an air of Elvis's 'All Shook Up' and echoes of Bill Haley, excellent for dancing and with lyrics that, although encouraging Chile and referring to its ceacheí, highlight football as a party between countries, the great Chilean hospitality and rock dance as a remedy for defeat."

– Spanish musician Igor Paskual

"World Cup anthems had none of the mass appeal back then: '*El Rock del Mundial*' is a fun and chirpy song that sounds like a Latin version of the rock staple 'Hound Dog', but there is nothing universal here. The song is all about the host nation Chile, and the band's lyrics function like parochial football commentary in certain parts: 'Get the rebound, goal, goal by Chile."

– World Cup anthems, who sang it best?', Saeed Saeed, *The National* (07/10/22)

2. World Cup Willie

First released: 1966
Highest UK chart position: N/A

England were on top of the world in 1966. Meanwhile, Lonnie Donegan's official anthem, 'World Cup Willie', was nestled somewhere outside the top 75. Talk about sleeping lions.

England saw the popularity of Chile's anthem and raised them a mascot. The success of the latter is evident in the fact that there has been a World Cup mascot every four years since, whereas official tournament songs didn't reoccur until 1990 and the two have never since been linked. Most football fans probably couldn't name Juanito (a boy wearing a sombrero — Mexico 1970), Naranjito (an orange in a football kit — Spain 1982), Ciao (a stick figure with a football head and a national flag tricolore body — Italy 1990) or La'eeb (a floating Arabic headdress with eyes and mouth — Qatar 2022), but they've been there, promoting every quadrennial tournament. English football supporters are probably more au fait with Gunnersaurus, Pete the Eagle and Filbert Fox, all of whom followed in Willie's wake.

Willie also spawned bedspreads, beer mats, tea towels, T-shirts, a comic strip and a multitude of general tat. The Football Association were remarkably far-sighted in recognising the potential of merchandising; Willie's creator, Reginald Hoye, was paid a one-off design fee, while the FA suits retained all commercial licensing rights. Hoye didn't mind. He was a freelance illustrator with Walter Tuckwell & Associates, who had been assigned the task of developing ideas for the official insignia, and it only took Hoye and his colleague Richard Culley five minutes to decide that a lion would work better than the initial idea of a bulldog in bowler hat or cloth cap — dismissed as too class-conscious — and a further five minutes for Reg to draw the roguish lion, based on his son Leo.

Hoye Jnr. has recalled: "Dad was excited because, at last, one of his artistic creations was coming to life. In addition to the fee, he got the odd perk, but I don't really think he wanted anything more than that."

Leo might not have been the only artistic muse: similarities have been cited in appearance and name to the FA's square-shouldered chief administrative officer, E. K. Willson, who would have been involved in negotiations concerning his look-/sound-alike. The resemblance between Willie's mane and the Beatles' mop-top haircuts has also drawn comment, aligning the king of beasts with Swinging Sixties music and fashions. Yet, despite the merchandising blitz, the music scene was strangely impervious to Willie's prowess.

The anomaly of World Cup Willie is that while the Four Lions (team + mascot) enjoyed unprecedented success, Lonnie Donegan's tie-in 45 tanked. How did 'Outstanding', the sole solo effort of moody Manchester United striker Andy Cole, chart higher (68) than a man revered by Lennon and McCartney? How is it possible that 'Gloryland', the anthem to USA '94, a tournament that had no Great British representative, performed better in the UK charts (36) than the official record accompanying England's home-soil triumph?

The answer, perhaps, is that the singer himself was a bit of an anomaly. Donegan was born in Glasgow to an Irish mother and

Scottish father but the family relocated to East Ham when little Lonnie was only two years old. The King of Skiffle's best-known song, 'My Old Man's a Dustman', exudes the kind of East End vibes World Cup heroes Moore, Hurst and Peters might have lapped up, although his most influential, 'Rock Island Line', has a more transnational flavour. However one looks at it, a Scots-born celebrity seems an incongruous choice to helm an English panegyric. Then again, Willie's waistcoat sports the Union Jack; with no other home nations qualifying for the 1966 World Cup, this might have been Hoye's or the FA's attempt at inclusion, although the more likely effect of such confederate thinking would have been to antagonise the Celts.

There's a degree of collective camaraderie in the lyrics, written by Syd Green who, unlike its singer, has little else to his credit. The first verse is a tad egotistical, introducing Willie and predicting that 'he'll be all the rage', its optimism propagated by the chorus's claim that Willie (symbolic of England of course, as indicated by the redundant simile 'he's tough as a lion') is 'favourite for the cup'. The second verse tones down the adulation and instead espouses the classic idea of a football family in the line that 'we're all so happy, like one big family' (try telling that to Chile and Italy). The third and final verse treads a fine line between being partisan and hospitable by proclaiming, 'All the fans are waiting / How they'll spur him on / And those 16 nations will soon know Willie's song'.

The brisk and bouncy brass orchestration by Tony Hatch (a close collaborator of Donegan's Pye labelmate Petula Clark and a prolific composer of TV themes, including *Neighbours*) goes some way to negating any sense of English arrogance, as does Donegan's chirpy persona. That said, the B-side 'Where in This World Are We Going?' might have better summed up Donegan's state of mind in 1966. Barely a decade earlier, pre-Elvis, Donegan had been cutting edge, his DIY rock the sound of the future; by the early Sixties, the hits had dried up and there was to be no Comeback Special, even with Willie roaring him on.

Jimmy Greaves could relate to feeling excluded from the party of '66; England's star striker was injured during the group stages and, despite regaining fitness, couldn't displace Geoff Hurst from the starting line-up. A man who rarely missed the mark, Greavsie's appraisal of the foundering 'World Cup Willie' suggests he would have been equally proficient as a music critic:

> "Lonnie was a great artist but it was a novelty song and only got patriotic airplay on BBC radio and not on pirate radio. Young kids just didn't relate to him. They were interested in the Beatles and the Rolling Stones."

Timing, it seems, is everything. And Donegan, who had been ahead of his time in the mid-Fifties, was out of time by the mid-Sixties. And having praised the FA for their foresight in readying Willie merchandise, the record producers perhaps paid the price for being a little too keen to cash in. 'World Cup Willie' was bizarrely released on 26 November 1965, long before Willie-mania set in and a full eight months ahead of the World Cup Final, when the record would have been expected to peak.

Still, flop record 'World Cup Willie' has more of a legacy than many major hits. The mascot's enduring popularity, propped up by the Three Lions' success and lent greater substance by every subsequent failure, means that the song has also endured. And Lonnie Donegan might not have been all the rage at the same time as Willie, but, with trends being cyclical, later generations have discovered the two in tandem. Ahead of South Africa 2010, Lonnie Donegan Jnr. gave the song a second lease of life with an Afrobeat tinge, and for Russia 2018, in the absence of an official England World Cup song for the first time since Willie's debut, streaming service Deezer urged fans to get behind the original.

The sweetest and most surreal tribute, however, came just a year after the event, in the Beatles' *Magical Mystery Tour* acid-fest, broadcast on Boxing Day 1967. George Claydon, the performer employed to embody Willie and who'd therefore spent the summer of '66 in a lion suit, was cast as Photographer George but was persuaded to don Willie's head once more in a subtle nod to the man who'd first inspired the Fab Four to pick up their instruments.

Reviews

"This song is irrevocably associated with England's greatest footballing moment."

– Lonnie Donegan Jnr.

"Possibly Donegan's worst record — although, perhaps, his residual talent removes it from football's absolute-worst list."

– 'The 11 worst football singles that should never have been committed to record', Anton Spice, thevinylfactory.com (12/06/14)

"Yes, it perhaps lacks the verve of a 'Waka Waka' but for its time, the ideation is commendably unique and the song is unavoidably adorable. As much as it may shock the Gen Z readers perusing through our selections, we're jumping on the 'World Cup Willie' bandwagon."

– Srinivas Sadhanand, Urban Pitch (07/10/22)

"I was seven in the summer of '66 and we had no TV so we used to walk round the corner to my aunt's house to watch the games. I still have my World Cup Willie badge and can remember all the words to the song 'Red, white and blue, World Cup Willie'. During the final I was very excited and fidgety and my dad kept telling me to sit still or leave the room!"

– David Lloyd, 'A People's History of 1966', *1966 and Not All That* (2016)

"World Cup Willie was a strange sort of lion who epitomised a nation in transition: On the one hand he was a vestige of male, Anglo-centric imperialism and on the other hand he was the cuddly symbol of a more democratic society. At its best, thanks to the likes of David Bowie and The Specials, the popular culture of which the tournament formed a part continued to be artistically innovative and socially challenging into the 1970s and beyond.

However, by the time England failed to qualify for the 1974 World Cup, the broad optimism of the '60s had turned into disillusionment."

– Richard Weight, 'This is England '66', *1966 and Not All That* (2016)

3. Back Home

First released: 1970
Highest UK chart position: 1

It's a paradox that a song by a bona fide music legend complementing a home-soil triumph should fail to even chart (see previous entry), while a song about a disappointing jaunt to Mexico by the underperformers who failed to bring the Jules Rimet Trophy back home should shoot to the top of the charts. The riddle is in part explained by the England World Cup squad of 1970 riding high off the back of 1966; eight of the eleven medal-winners were still going strong and perhaps the enthusiastic record-buying public were compensating for neglecting 'World Cup Willie'.

On this occasion, England's official song probably benefited from an early release, albeit only two months in advance rather than an epic eight — record label Pye had clearly learnt their lesson. Released on 12 April 1970, a large dose of pre-tournament optimism helped 'Back Home' to hit number one on 16 May, two weeks before England's first group match with Romania; by the time the ball slipped through Peter Bonetti's gloves, helping to set up West

Germany's revenge, the record had slipped to number three. Oddly, ardent admirers kept it in the charts for a further two months, notching up 17 weeks in total.

There is an entrenched patriotism which states that the English national team shouldn't employ outsiders. Yet long before the managerial reins were handed to Sven-Göran Eriksson (subject of an ode by comedy duo Bell & Spurling, 'Sven Sven Sven', rush-released to commemorate the 5-1 away thrashing of old enemy Germany during 2002 World Cup qualifying) and tuneless Fabio Capello (the strict Italian reportedly rejected big-name overtures for a 2010 World Cup anthem as he feared it being a distraction, but Dizzee Rascal and James Corden went ahead and released Tears for Fears rejig 'Shout' anyway), Lonnie Donegan, Phil Coulter and Bill Martin were employed to choreograph the musical support. Donegan's Scots-Irish ancestry was duplicated in the songwriting partnership of Coulter (Derry, Northern Ireland) and Martin (born William Wylie Macpherson in Sir Alex Ferguson's stomping ground of Govan).

Like the skiffle merchant before them and foreign managers after, Coulter and Martin brought prestige. The English FA took their lead from the Eurovision jury in selecting a champion; Coulter and Martin had penned Sandie Shaw's 'Puppet on a String', which took first place at the Eurovision Song Contest 1967, and Cliff Richard's 'Congratulations', which was runner-up the year after. Both songs had also topped the UK singles chart.

Coulter and Martin also won multiple Ivor Novello Awards, but they didn't do anything particularly innovative with 'Back Home' save perhaps making it so bland as to be chorus-less. Coulter's simple music hall melody is overlaid with Martin's mawkish lyrics, carolled by a bunch of bullish young men off to give their all for the glory of their nation. Unsurprisingly, the end result has the haunting air of a song from the trenches of the First or Second World War:

Back home, they'll be thinking about us
When we are far away

The intention was to give an uplifting *au revoir* to the fans, to fortify the bond between team and home. In practice, the England World Cup Squad 1970 (as the artists were credited on the record sleeve) sound like hesitant soldiers who'd rather be with their sweethearts than taking shots at the Germans. They do their best to keep their ends up and voices cheerful but there's no tubthumping; football and war have become grievously equated in the English psyche, yet contrary to all the imperialistic bombast that emanates from the terraces, 'Back Home' doesn't even make explicit mention of being reigning world champions. Instead, it's rather deferential:

> Back home, though they think we're the greatest
> That's what we've got to prove
> Once more we will meet with the best
> Once more we'll be put to the test

No more being 'sensation[s] of the age' and 'everybody's favourite for the cup', even though 1970 was the last time England credibly entered a tournament as favourites. Rather, it all feels a bit of an ordeal, defeated before even sallying forth. Are Coulter and Martin to blame for the fatalism that has stalked the England men's team ever since?

The World Beaters Sing the World Beaters would suggest not! If self-adulation is lacking in 'Back Home', it appears two-fold in the title of the accompanying LP, in which the squad take on the hits of Coulter and Martin plus an assortment of Sixties family favourites ('Sugar, Sugar', 'Lily the Pink', 'Ob-La-Di, Ob-La-Da') and a token patriotic anthem ('There'll Always Be an England'). Bobby Moore might have been wrongfully arrested in the Bogotá Bracelet incident, but he could legitimately have been hauled up sooner for crimes against music. Still, hitting a few bum notes didn't stop the England captain's lead vocals on 'Sugar, Sugar' being proudly recycled on West Ham compilation *Forever Blowing Bubbles* (1997), credited to Bobby Moore & Friends. Nor did the suspect harmonising stop *The World Beaters* reaching the top five in the album charts. And if you can't enjoy Norman Hunter and Terry Cooper butchering a Beatles' novelty song then really, what are you even doing here?

Album track and 7" B-side 'Cinnamon Stick' was certainly enjoyed by David Baddiel and Frank Skinner. The erstwhile flatmates had already resurrected 'Back Home' (astonishingly not as old then as 'Three Lions' is now) by taking its melody as the focal point to the title music for their off-the-wall comedy vehicle *Fantasy Football League*. The end credits, meanwhile, resurrected Jeff Astle's singing career. The former West Brom striker and Skinner's boyhood idol would trot out at the end of each episode to gamely lead the guests in an improbable rendition of some seemingly random song, typically tenuously linked to what had gone before.

Astle had manifestly been one of the more enthusiastic and capable members of the World Beaters, assuming sole lead vocals on Vera Lynn standard 'You're in My Arms', and he presumably spent longer in the recording studio than the 85 minutes he spent on the pitch in Mexico. A year later he also released a commendable solo single, 'Sweet Water'. Now, even though *Fantasy Football* was generally more erudite than its late-night contributions to Nineties lad culture might suggest, the innuendo-laced lyrics of 'Cinnamon Stick' — 'Sweet as sugar, nice as pie / Cinnamon stick, cinnamon stick / See that twinkle in her eye / Cinnamon stick, cinnamon stick' — provided an open goal and Astle duly performed the cult favourite that had been a suspect duet between Brian Labone and Francis Lee on the 1970 original. Capitalising on the King of West Bromwich's newfound popularity, RPM Records, specialists in 1960s-1980s compilations, reissued *The World Beaters Sing the World Beaters* as *Jeff Astle and the 1970 World Cup Squad Sing!!*. Sadly, Astle's revival would be short lived; signs of the dementia caused by the repeated heading of heavy leather footballs was already beginning to show as he struggled to remember lyrics. Astle died in 2002, aged 59, but the Jeff Astle Foundation has been instrumental in confronting the neurodegenerative diseases that have afflicted numerous other members of the 1970 World Cup Squad and many more players of his generation.

Hyperbolic claims have been made for the gloom that arose from England's inglorious quarter-final exit at the 1970 World Cup helping to topple Harold Wilson's Labour government a few days later. Taking a longer view, it could be seen as a microcosmic allegory of Britain's decline versus Germany's emergence as a football and economic powerhouse. Where Britain did remain strong throughout the latter part of the 20th century, however, was in the soft power of pop culture, and the England squad of 1970 can at least take a bow for setting the template for team singalongs that brought us 'Blue is the Colour', 'Marching on Together' and many, many more.

Reviews

"Alf [Ramsey] didn't really disapprove but he didn't know how to sell it so he suggested I meet up with 'the boys' and it would be up to them. I met up with the team before they travelled to a match in Belgium. I promised them a No 1 gold disc and an appearance on *Top of the Pops*. The rest is history!"

– music impresario Bill Martin on selling the song to the squad

"When some genius in the record company asked the question 'But can they sing?', the answer was, it doesn't matter. We weren't counting on their vocal prowess, we were banking on their popularity as soccer stars ... Every time England won a game, we sold another truckload of records. I was thinking to myself, if they win this, we could sell millions upon millions of records and I could buy a house in the Caribbean, maybe even retire ... [When England lost to West Germany] I picked up my dinner and threw it at the TV!"

– co-writer Phil Coulter quoted by *The Morning Star* 50 years after the event

"Jeff Astle was one of the shockingly few footballers actually I really liked, despite the fact he didn't play for Liverpool. He was also notable for being one of the few footballers — I used to hate it when he was patronised by Skinner and Baddiel on that programme they used to do, I used to find that really irritating — but he was also one of the few footballers, as I was about to say, who made a half-decent record [in 'Sweet Water']."

– John Peel on Radio 1

"He loved singing, Jeff. He used to sing in the church choir. And he loved making the record 'Back Home'. Suited and booted for *Top of the Pops* — I can still visualise it. Singers at the front, grunters went at the back! The silver disc is hanging up at home, pride of place."

– Laraine Astle, widow of Jeff, June 2023

4. Ally's Tartan Army

First released: 1978
Highest UK chart position: 6

Scottish World Cup songs fluctuate wildly between shameless self-belief and shamefaced resignation.

The latter is typified by Del Amitri's 'Don't Come Home Too Soon' (1998), which makes England's 'This Time (We'll Get It Right)' — the 1982 follow-up to 'Back Home' reflecting on successive failures to qualify — sound positively buoyant. If William Wallace had delivered such modest (some might say honest) rhetoric before the Battle of Stirling Bridge, Scottish history would be markedly less stirring. Sample lyrics:

> So long, go on and do your best
> Let all France have whiskey on its breath
> The world may not be shaking yet
> But you might prove them wrong
> Even long shots make it

In terms of consistency, Scotland had outperformed England by qualifying for five successive World Cups between 1974 and 1990.

Sadly, their consistency extended to not getting beyond the group stage in any of their previous seven efforts. The self-deprecating pragmatism of singer-songwriter Justin Currie, who proffers that anything better than this can be considered a success, chimed with a large enough proportion of the population that the song reached number one in the Official Scottish Chart and 15 in the UK-wide countdown. Those wanting a bit more *Braveheart*, however (the Oscar-winning Mel Gibson film had been released in 1995 and stoked Scottish nationalism), were less impressed. Despite singing 'I don't care what people say', in an interview publicising Del Amitri's 2021 album *Fatal Mistake*, Currie named allowing the song to be used as Scotland's official anthem his biggest life regret: "I got an absolute pounding for that song not being sufficiently jingoistic and triumphalist enough, so yeah, I regret doing that."

Currie might not have had all of the Tartan Army behind him, but he could at least count on the players. The squad provide backing vocals and some of the most rugged (namely Colin Hendry, Christian Dailly and Gordon Durie) feature in the video's airport kickabout with fans. Suffice to say, they came home early, having gained one point and finished bottom of a group containing Brazil, Norway and Morocco.

The moroseness of the late-Nineties should, however, have been forgivable after the misplaced hubris of the Seventies.

Kicking off with 'Easy, Easy', the 1974 World Cup squad's statement of intent was not exactly easy listening but appealed to children hooked in by the Flintstone-style holler of 'Yabba-dabba-do, we support the boys in blue and it's easy, easy'. It was composed by the same person who came up with 'Shang-a-Lang' by tartan-clad teenybopper heartthrobs the Bay City Rollers. And that person was none other than Bill Martin, who it turns out hadn't been saving his best for his native Scotland when the Auld Enemy called in 1970. Martin ought to have been well versed in the language of football, having played professionally for Rangers. Johannesburg Rangers, in South Africa, that is. He also played for the illustrious youth club

Blantyre Celtic and had trials with Partick Thistle, but his ease with both ball and words seems to have been lost in translation. 'Easy, Easy' was strangely prophetic, however. Scotland were undefeated at the 1974 World Cup but still went out on goal difference at the group stage having only put two past Zaire, whereas Yugoslavia and Brazil notched nine and three respectively; Willie Ormond's men were retrospectively criticised for taking it easy and retaining possession rather than pressing home their advantage.

Regardless of the early exit, being the only undefeated team in 1974 must have gone to their heads. National self-esteem was also bolstered by being the best the United Kingdom had to offer. Under the charge of Ally MacLeod, Scotland won the 1976-77 Home International Championship, with the jubilant Tartan Army famously collapsing the crossbar after the decisive game at Wembley. From the same school of modesty as José Mourinho, the manager announced at his unveiling as national boss, "My name is Ally MacLeod, and I'm a winner". If that sounds like someone rebuffing an AA meeting, later pronouncements sound like the result of heavy intoxication.

Jock Stein had been first choice for the job, but that didn't dent MacLeod's confidence as he proceeded to claim that a friendly with Brazil was a trial run for the World Cup Final. When asked what he planned to do after winning the World Cup, he replied sharply, "Retain it"! *The Guardian* described him as the "Pied Piper of the Scottish game" and the fans were dancing to MacLeod's tune when more than 30,000 turned up at Hampden to witness a rapturous send-off that more closely resembled a victory parade, with ten massed pipe bands taking to the field and an open-top bus circling the pitch. Stein sounded a note of cogent caution when he remarked that it was all well and good "turning handstands" at qualifying for a World Cup that England had failed to reach, but "there's a big world out there and the English aren't the only people who live in it".

Blatantly ignoring the wisdom of the Celtic doyen, into this melee marched comedian and Rangers fan Andy Cameron. Cameron had entered showbusiness in the early-Seventies, making a name for himself on the comedy circuit with a football hooligan act. In 1975 he dipped a toe into the music industry by writing and recording 'The Greatest Team of All', about his beloved Rangers. Setting aside local rivalries for national ones, he followed this up in 1978 with the self-aggrandising stomp of 'Ally's Tartan Army':

> We're on the march with Ally's Army
> We're going to the Argentine
> And we'll really shake them up
> When we win the World Cup
> Coz Scotland are the greatest football team

The tune came from the American Civil War song 'Tramp! Tramp! Tramp!', which has been re-versioned by numerous sets of fans, not least the Irish, who had already adapted the melody to create Irish nationalist anthem 'God Save Ireland', which then formed the backbone of the Republic of Ireland's 1990 World Cup song 'Put 'Em Under Pressure', which stole Cameron's chorus almost verbatim save swapping 'Ally's Army' for 'Jackie's', 'Argentine' for 'Italy' and 'Scotland' for 'Ireland'.

Boastful chorus aside, Ireland's version (produced by U2's Larry Mullen Jnr. no less) thrives on an aggressive underdog spirit, whereas Cameron's verses double-down on the braggadocio by comparing Ally MacLeod to Muhammad Ali, promising to show the world a whole new brand of football, and rubbing salt in England's wounds ('We're representing Britain, we've got to do or die / For England cannae do it coz they didnae qualify' — credit to songwriter Samuel Dennison).

'Ally's Tartan Army' sold 360,000 copies and reached the UK top ten, with the uncouth Andy Cameron twice appearing on *Top of the Pops* alongside Kate Bush and Blondie. But pride comes before a fall. Hoping to capitalise on Scotland's World Cup fever, Cameron poured his projected royalties into producing 'Andy's Tartan Album', which sank without trace as the Tartan Army returned home with their tails between their legs. Archie Gemmill's wonder-goal in a victory over the Netherlands showed what could have been, had the boys in blue not already lost to Peru and drawn with Iran. In Dundee, one record shop slashed the price of 'Ally's Tartan Army' from 65p to 1p and urged disappointed customers to buy in bulk and smash the vinyl singles with a hammer.

MacLeod resigned one match later, returning to the second tier of Scottish football with Ayr United, where he had first made his name in management. The Scottish Football Association's annual report read:

> "Regardless of the depressing aspects of Mr MacLeod's latter days in the Association's employ, it would be quite unfair not to comment that he was largely responsible for kindling an enthusiasm for the Scottish team that far exceeded anything that had gone before."

Also getting Scotland mixed up with Brazil in '78 was Rod Stewart. 'Ole, Ola (Mulher Brasileira)', the official Scotland World Cup song, eschewed guitars and bagpipes for tamborims and shakers. Over the top of this samba sound, Rod's raspy vocal confidently intoned, 'We're gonna bring that World Cup back from over there'. Conflating an Argentinian World Cup with Brazilian rhythms is probably as insulting as thinking Scotland is in England, but then the closest 'Ole, Ola' gets to humility is accepting the Germans might be a challenge and wishing right-back Danny McGrain — the first Protestant to play for Celtic and subject of 'Sliding In (Like McGrain)', a 1996 song by Glaswegian rock band Big Wednesday — wasn't injured.

The title translates as 'Hey, Hey (Brazilian Woman)' and is an adaptation of '*Mulher à Brasileira*' (Woman in Brazil), written by Evaldo Gouveia and Jair Amorim. The single is Scottified by a tartan cover featuring Stewart clutching a beer bottle. B-side 'I'd Walk a Million Miles for One of Your Goals' is not an attempt at surpassing the Proclaimers but it does rival Andy Cameron B-side 'Ah Want Tae Be a Punk Rocker' for added eccentricity, being a mash-up of 'Que Sera, Sera' and 'My Mammy' (featuring the line 'I'd walk a million miles for one of your smiles', from whence the title is contrived). Sir Rod Stewart, as he is now, has shrugged off '*Ole, Ola*' as "whimsical", but it caught the wave of Scottish triumphalism, charting two places higher than 'Ally's Tartan Army' at number four.

Rod returned for Euro '96, by which point the Scottish FA had clearly decided to keep things simple and understated. 'Purple Heather', also known as 'Wild Mountain Thyme' and 'Will Ye Go, Lassie, Go?', is a Scottish folk song dating from the early-19th century and had appeared on Stewart's seventeenth studio album, *A Spanner in the Works* (1995), before being co-opted for patriotic soccer purposes. Special mention too to 'The Big Man and the Scream Team Meet the Barmy Army Uptown', an unofficial Euro '96 collaboration between Primal Scream, *Trainspotting* author Irvine Welsh and dub specialist Adrian Sherwood's On-U Sound. It came with a "Warning: this record is offensive" sticker; anyone familiar with Bobby Gillespie and Irvine Welsh will understand why. And finally, kudos to 'We Have a Dream' for its tacit admission that football songs don't care for powerhouse vocals, instead employing a dramatic spoken word narrative and shouty chorus performed by the 1982 World Cup Squad and John Gordon Sinclair, reprising his role from *Gregory's Girl* (1981) as an awkward fantasist.

Reviews

"It was just a laugh. I thought *Top of the Pops* was a wind-up. When I phoned my father asking for a lift to the studio he thought the same. So there I was under all these lights, 38 years old, sweating in my kilt, tammy, Lion Rampant over my shoulders and waiting on my big moment when along comes Billy Idol of Generation X. 'Who the f**k are you?' he said. My father was going to hit him. He had to be held back by my brothers."

– Andy Cameron in *The Scotsman*, 6 March 2021

"It just made us feel like we were invincible. We were not only gonnae go to Argentina and win the World Cup, we were on *Top of the Pops*. What more do you want?"

– broadcaster Grant Stott, *Scotland's Football Jukebox*, BBC Scotland at the Euros (2021)

"As a kid, the 1978 World Cup in Argentina, there was no England team, I supported Scotland. I was ten years old. And in fact my first single I ever bought was 'Ally's Tartan Army'."

– Radiohead guitarist Ed O'Brien speaking to Scottish broadcaster Edith Bowman before headlining Glasgow's TRNSMT Festival 2017

"A fun tune wae that same sorta caleidgh style beat as the rest. Some great references tae Muhamed Ali n Pele which is telling ae it's time. Ah'm anticipatin' this song bein' oan in the pub jukey when ah get doon there."

– Jamie Keenan, drummer and vocalist of Motherwell rockers the LaFontaines reviewing past Scotland anthems for *Clash* magazine to promote their own effort, 'Scotland, Bonnie Scotland' (2021)

5. World in Motion

First released: 1990
Highest UK chart position: 1

'We ain't no hooligans, this ain't a football song'

The Channel 4 documentary *Italia '90: When Football Changed Forever* (2022) depicted the last World Cup before the formation of the Premier League as a watershed moment for the beautiful game, when hooliganism gave way to family-friendly entertainment, transformed by proactive policing and Gazza's tears acting as some kind of magic PR balm. This is a somewhat simplistic narrative, but if it's going to be told then it needs a chapter on The Greatest Football Song of All Time™.

English football was indeed at a low ebb in the late-Eighties. Club sides had been banned from European football since the 1985 Heysel disaster, when a breaching of the stadium segregation by Liverpool fans resulted in the death of 39 Juventus fans. With disturbing talk of score settling between Italian ultras and English firms, there was genuine concern that Italia '90 was shaping up to be a diplomatic nightmare and that an international injunction would surely follow.

Things weren't looking a lot better on the musical front. In 1986, 'We've Got the Whole World at Our Feet' stumbled to the apt chart position of 66, with the uncharitable *NME* describing it as the England squad "barking over a cheesy Casio keyboard factory preset". Even worse, its long-form companion, *World Cup Party*, contained B-side 'When We Are Far From Home' (a retread of previous themes) and a series of interminable medleys with a vague geographical nexus that dared to pair Hoddle and Waddle with 'The Lion Sleeps Tonight'. Come 1988, even the late-Eighties hit factory of Stock, Aitken and Waterman couldn't produce anything better than 'All the Way', which was even more forgettable than England's pointless European Championship. The vogueish genres of synth-pop and rap seemed far removed from the rock 'n' roll of the Sixties and the glam stomp of the Seventies that lent themselves more readily to football singalongs.

Enter New Order. *Low-Life* (1985) had not been a treatise on the knuckle-scraping thuggery of the Millwall Bushwackers, nor did 'Touched by the Hand of God' (1987) have anything to do with Maradona. Lead vocalist Bernard Sumner has admitted to being in no position to write football-inspired lyrics and drummer Stephen Morris recounts the bemused reaction when Factory Records supremo Tony Wilson first floated the idea of a World Cup song: "When I stopped laughing, I realised he might be serious."

In typical Tony Wilson style (check out 2002 film *24 Hour Party People* if you don't already know the legend behind the man), Morris speculated to *The Independent* in 2010, "Knowing Tony, he probably sold them the idea of us doing a song and then told us the FA had come up with the brilliant idea". According to most sources however, the man we have to thank for making the link is FA press officer David Bloomfield.

Far more down with the kids than 75-year-old FA chairman Bert Millichip, Bloomfield was on a mission to break the mould. He took as his blueprint 'The Official Colourbox World Cup Theme', by alternative electronic group Colourbox from the 4AD label (home of

Cocteau Twins, Dead Can Dance and Pixies). Colourbox disbanded in 1987, but not before collaborating with A. R. Kane to create seminal dancefloor smash 'Pump Up the Volume' under the guise of M|A|R|R|S. Their pulsing *Doctor Who*-esque 'World Cup Theme' had been written for that nominal purpose, in the hope that it would be used by BBC's *Grandstand* for the Mexico 1986 World Cup. That honour went instead to the not dissimilar 'Aztec Lightning' by Heads. Noticing that wilfully obscure Radio 1 DJ John Peel would sometimes play American football songs, Bloomfield wanted an English soccer song that would pass Peel's quality control check.

New Order came into the frame when Bloomfield spied that they had provided the title music to *Best and Marsh: The Perfect Match* (1988), an eight-part reminiscence on George Best and Rodney Marsh's Seventies heyday, compered by Tony Wilson, fulfilling his TV industry role as producer/presenter for Granada (the north-west branch of ITV). The track 'Best and Marsh' also appeared as the B-side to 1989 single 'Round & Round'. Tales of the negotiations between FA and Factory vary according to teller, but the version told by bassist Peter Hook to *GQ Sport* on the song's 20th anniversary is perhaps the best and most believable:

> "[Wilson] was at a football do and the PR team from the FA was there. He [Bloomfield] was telling Tony what a fan he was of New Order and Factory Records and he said, 'God, I wish I could get them to do the World Cup song.' So Tony said, 'Well, why don't you f**king ask them then?' It was as simple as that."

Musically, the band took a shortcut. True to the lyric 'when something's good it's never gone', the backing rhythm was taken wholesale from another TV theme, this time for the BBC's current affairs youth programme *Reportage* which, though credited to New Order, had been composed by Stephen Morris and keyboardist Gillian Gilbert as The Other Two, a name which referred to the fact that the better-known Sumner (Electronic) and Hook (Ad Infinitum and Revenge) had already embarked on side projects.

For help with the lyrics, they signed up actor and agent provocateur Keith Allen (dad of Lily and Alfie), who hung out at the Factory-owned Manchester superclub the Haçienda before moving upmarket to London's Groucho Club, where he drunkenly collided with Blur bassist Alex James and Young British Artist Damien Hirst to create Fat Les's 'Vindaloo' (1998), a half-arsed yet surprisingly well-received attempt at harnessing a laddish football chant into song form. Taking his cue from the FA's sole stipulation, that the song mustn't reference hooliganism, Allen's first input was to take a binary opposite approach inspired by the Haçienda's famously loved-up atmosphere:

E is for England
England starts with E
We'll all be smiling
When we're in Italy

This proposed chorus was vetoed by the FA, who recognised the overt references to ecstasy, the party drug that had Middle England in a moral panic during the Second Summer of Love, sparked by the illegal rave culture. The authorities failed to detect, however, a more subtle reference to the ecstasy pill — 'it's one on one' — which conveniently works as both a coaching manoeuvre and an allusion to the acid house expression 'are you on one?'! The nucleus of Allen's loved-up mindset also remains in the titular call to arms, 'Love's got the world in motion'. The FA politely asked if it could be changed to 'We've got the world in motion' but, citing the original anti-hooligan brief, the band refused their paymaster's request. The pop canon is chock-a-block with songs about love, so retaining that one word shouldn't constitute a revolutionary act, yet those four little letters make a world of difference and get to the heart of the song, giving it a universality that the self-absorbed 'we've' (so much more typical of tribal football songs) would've stolen. After all, 'this ain't a football song'.

If Allen was 'on one', the players' drug of choice was alcohol. The recording took place during an international fixture week; with

Brazil visiting on the Wednesday, Bobby Robson gave his players leave on the Sunday to attend the recording. Most of them went to the pub instead. And the half-dozen who did head to the Mill studio in Berkshire were not model professionals. Philip Shotton, director of the music video, was amused by the scene that greeted him: "We went down to the studio at about half 10 in the morning and the first thing we saw was Gazza moonwalking with a glass of champagne in his hand. We just thought, 'This is going to be f**king brilliant.'"

American producer Stephen Hague was nonplussed by the chaos surrounding him. Gazza was equally nonplussed by the mixing desk, allegedly declaring, "Aye, that's a big organ"! And the players were surprised by New Order's presence, having not been told who was involved. The expectation, according to John Barnes, was that they'd turn up and sing something along the lines of 'Here we go, here we go, here we go'. Then they bumped into the people behind the biggest-selling 12" single of all time ('Blue Monday' has shifted more than three million units, though the original 1983 pressing notoriously ran at a loss because of the high production costs behind Peter Saville's intricate sleeve design). Morris told *GQ*, "The football team thought football songs were s**t as well. So they basically had to be blackmailed into turning up". Hook was intrigued by Wilson handing each player an envelope of cash, on which Barnes expounds, "We earned about £200 each for the players' pool ... we should have gone for the royalties!"

Joining Gazza and Barnes in providing backing vocals and getting stuck into a fridge of champagne were Des Walker, Chris Waddle, Peter Beardsley and Steve McMahon. Gary Lineker was a notable absentee; the 1986 Golden Boot winner was reportedly readying his own release, 'If We Win It All', which, perhaps for the good of his unsullied image, never saw the light of day. Memories are a bit hazy, probably from all the booze consumed, but at some point in proceedings, a rap-off ensued ...

Barnes told *CNN*, "After a while, and a few glasses of wine, someone drunkenly said 'Why don't we just put a rap in it?'"

Morris divulged to *FourFourTwo* that it was a more premeditated move to guard against critical and commercial failure: "If it all went pear-shaped, at least we could say it was a joke." Allen was chief instigator but his ideas were only half-formed. Eventual B-side (ingenuously titled 'The B-Side') is the song in demo form, with Allen's "naff football chants and JB impersonation" (as credited on the sleeve) in place of the players' input. (Upping the cool quotient, in-demand DJs also provided alternative mixes, such as the Subbuteo Dub by Graeme Park and Mike Pickering, and the Carabinieri Mix by Andrew Weatherall and Terry Farley, which does use the rejected hook of 'We've got the world in motion' but is also named after the Italian gendarmerie, thus keeping the jingoism in check.)

Once Allen had cobbled together the final words, the next question was, who was going to perform the rap? Gazza was apparently the most natural and tuneful MC, but also the most unintelligible. Strong regional accents also counted against Waddle, Beardsley and McMahon. Master tapes of the "unheard England raps", described by Omega Auctions as "comedy gold", sold for £500 in October 2021; fortunately for all those who missed the auction, the outtakes are available on YouTube. Barnes easily prevailed over Walker in the final rap battle and a legend was born. JB had been spitting rhymes from the Sugarhill Gang since his teens, while Public Enemy and N.W.A. had made waves in the Eighties, yet for a generation of middle-class white children, 'You've got to hold and give' was their first exposure to the rap genre that came to dominate youth culture. Barnes is frequently asked to recreate his tour de force, including by pop phenomenon Ed Sheeran, who posted their collaboration on Instagram alongside the comment "John Barnes $wag". In an interview with *Soccer AM* in 2009, Peter Hook revealed that there had been plans for David Beckham to step into Barnes's boots for a 2002 re-release but, having given the band virtual free rein with the original, the FA sensibly prohibited this.

The final contributor was Kenneth Wolstenholme, who was persuaded to re-record his indelible commentary from the 1966

World Cup Final. As well as sidestepping the headache of licensing, Wolstenholme's words were also changed from "Some people are on the pitch" to "Some of the crowd are on the pitch" because it scanned better. The use of commentary over the intro would be copied on 'Three Lions', whose architects might also have noted the first recorded reference to the three lions passant guardant adorning the national crest.

Issued under the moniker ENGLANDneworder, Bernard Sumner said to the *NME* at the time of release, "This should be the last straw for Joy Division fans." It's unclear if he was alluding specifically to the association with association football, or the band's musical evolution from post-punk to post-rave, made all the more pertinent by this utterance coming almost a decade to the day from the suicide of Ian Curtis, magnetic frontman of the proto-goths from whose embers New Order grew. Joy Division's throbbing debut album 'Unknown Pleasures' bore the catalogue number FACT 10. FAC 293 was Factory Records one and only number one single, climbing to the top spot the day after Italia '90 kicked off, thereby setting the tone for English football's renaissance. It was unable, however, to prevent the label from hurtling towards bankruptcy, which is in part explained by FAC 295 being a Christmas greetings card and FAC 331 being a floating boardroom table. Factory wasn't just a record label, it was a modern art installation. Likewise, 'World in Motion' was never just a football song.

Reviews

"We had to get a comedian and a football team in to [get a number one], so if anybody else wants to know how to get a hit record, there's a tip."

– career advice from New Order's Stephen Morris

"Every time the World Cup comes around people talk about it, which shows how iconic the song was. It wasn't a typical 'here we go', arms-around-each-other football song. It was a proper group. I got a little kudos from it, but the song was really just a great song by New Order."

– John Barnes speaking to *The Independent* in 2018

"England was another sporting country in 1990. English football wasn't hip. It wasn't a cultural monolith that swallowed whole newspaper sports sections, leaving other games gasping for air. Football certainly wasn't anything to do with rock'n'roll, except in the most embarrassing ways. Though George Best had once been considered Beatle-like, and the Kinks would cancel gigs to watch Arsenal, those associations were ancient history. New Order's 'World in Motion' single was the first indication that everything was about to change."

– Nick Hasted, *The Independent* (2018)

"The best part of any song is John Barnes's rap."

– Ed Sheeran on *That Peter Crouch Podcast*, June 2021

6. Nessun Dorma

First released: 1926
Highest UK chart position: 2

If football and opera initially seemed even stranger bedfellows than ENGLANDneworder, it's only because the general public seemed strangely ignorant of the stirring melodrama that's inherent in the English game until BSkyB joined forces with the Premier League to exploit it. First, however, to treat football with the operatic flourish it occasionally deserves was the BBC's coverage of the Italia '90 World Cup. And if David Bloomfield was the visionary who saw that an England anthem could be more than just a standard football song, it was young editor and producer Philip Bernie who bridged the gap between high and low culture and made Luciano Pavarotti a household name.

The aria, from the final act of Giacomo Puccini's *Turandot*, was trialled on the tense but rather less emotive World Cup draw. "In 1989, I was cutting various montages for the World Cup draw," says Bernie, "and around that time I heard '*Nessun Dorma*' played on *Desert Island Discs*. After using it for the draw, I suggested using it for the titles music and it all evolved from there." If the picking of the balls could be rendered operatic, then the kicking of them would be breathtakingly climactic.

The iconic image of Marco Tardelli's fist-pumping goal celebration from Italy's 1982 Final victory, which would be the closing shot of the title sequence, was Bernie's starting point. He became fixated on this due to its visual correspondence with the aria's rousing aural refrain of '*vincerò*', meaning 'I will win'. "[It] was the crucial shot for the finale — mouth agape to mirror Pavarotti's voice," Bernie explained to Irish sports outlet *The42* (Tardelli was the Republic of Ireland's assistant manager for five years under Giovanni Trapattoni, which would be enough to explain Irish interest even if 1990 hadn't also been their best performance in a major championship).

The slow build to the musical and emotional apex also appealed to Bernie: "It is a very powerful but a quite slow-tempo theme and at that time, themes were generally fast and high-tempo." Most sports themes were cheap, low-grade library music, although the BBC had pushed the boat out for the previous three World Cups. For Argentina '78 they commissioned West End whizz Andrew Lloyd-Webber, presumably off the back of *Evita* (the original rock opera concept album was released in 1976 and its first theatrical run coincided with that World Cup), to write 'Argentine Melody (*Canción de Argentina*)'. Indicating the mirth with which it was treated, however, the theme was performed by Rod Argent (once of the Zombies) under the alias San Jose featuring **Rod**riguez **Argent**ina. (Argent would also supply ITV's long-forgotten Italia '90 theme, '*Tutti Al Mondo*'.) For Spain '82, the BBC licensed an existing Lloyd-Webber composition, 'The Jellicle Ball' from Cats, which had brought T. S. Eliot's light poetry to the stage the year before. And for Mexico '86 they used Heads' 'Aztec Lightning', which helped get Bloomfield thinking ...

If previous titles had incorporated a small degree of artistry, Bernie took things higher by producing a sequence in the grand style of Cicero. Beginning with an extreme close-up of Italian Renaissance art accompanied by an angelic choir fading in as if descending from on high, the curtains then rise on an interpretive dance representation of Silvio Gazzaniga's golden World Cup Trophy sculpture. Having clearly aligned football with art, we then have a graphically stylised slow-motion montage of past and present greats including Pelé, Cruyff, Maradona and Klinsmann, leading to the glorious crescendo of brass, tenor and Tardelli.

The victorious Tardelli was cast in the role of Calaf. For readers who don't know the difference between *Turandot* and Arda Turan, Puccini's opera is based loosely on an epic poem from 12th century Persia and revolves around the story of Prince Calaf, the cocksure suitor of Princess Turandot (whereas Turan is a Turkish football manager who used to play for Barcelona). The eponymous princess is emotionally distant and deters suitors with three riddles that they must solve to win her hand; get any wrong and they are beheaded. That's the metaphor for knockout football. Calaf passes the test but Turandot reneges on the terms set and refuses to marry him. In response, Calaf sets her a test: if she correctly guesses his name then she can execute him; if she fails to do so then she must marry. This act is the equivalent of extra time. At the penalty shootout stage, Turandot orders her subjects to discover his name and if they fail to do so then their forfeit is death. And this is where '*Nessun Dorma*' (None Shall Sleep) comes in. An aria is a self-contained piece for one voice, and in the moonlit palace gardens a gloating Calaf sings of his imminent victory.

The sound recording used by the BBC was from 1972, conducted by Zubin Mehta and performed by the London Philharmonic Orchestra and a 36-year-old Luciano Pavarotti. The young Luciano loved farming and football more than anything else. The impulse to sing professionally sprang from Llangollen, Wales, where the male voice choir he and his father were part of claimed first prize at the 1955 International Eisteddfod. He debuted at the Royal Opera House, Covent Garden in 1965 and his star continued to rise in the world of opera, but the name Pavarotti was little known outside of these circles. As Calaf states to Princess Turandot immediately before the aria, '*Il mio nome non sai*' (My name you do not know).

Record label Decca were initially resistant to the BBC's usage and the equation of a niche yet respected music artist with the uncultured world of football. Rival label Epic stole a march on them by releasing their own version of 'Nessun Dorma' by Plácido Domingo in early June, but this 'unofficial' version failed to break the top 40. Pavarotti's recording entered the charts at 21 on 16 June and, in the words of Bernie: "It just took off. It was greatly helped by how England did. The record company were very pleased how it turned out."

By the time England played Cameroon in the quarter-final, Pavarotti had risen above ENGLANDneworder and only Elton John stood in the way of a football one-two in the UK music charts. With more than 25 million tuning in to watch England's semi-final against West Germany on BBC1, Pavarotti and opera were being exposed to a larger audience than ever before. And the impact stretched far beyond these shores. On the eve of the 1990 World Cup Final, Pavarotti joined forces with José Carreras and Plácido Domingo to perform as the Three Tenors for the first time, in a concert from the ancient Roman Baths of Caracalla that was beamed to a global television audience of approximately 800 million. They would also perform at the next three World Cup Finals and the concert recording went three times platinum in the US and became the best-selling opera record in history. Follow-ups, including a 1998 Three Tenors recording of 'You'll Never Walk Alone', failed to hit the same heights, but Pavarotti enjoyed pop star status throughout the Nineties, performing live with the likes of Bono and the Spice Girls.

The image of Tardelli might have been the inception but for most viewers the definitive accompaniment to 'Nessun Dorma' is Gazza's tears on realising that he wouldn't be gracing the final, a show of emotion that encapsulated the changing face of English football. Unlike Calaf, victory was not his. He would, however, carry the flame of Italia '90 into the next phase of his career.

The thunderous '*vincerò*' reverberates in the title music to *Gazzetta Football Italia* and its distinctive '*Golaccio*' climax.

Pre-Premier League, Italy's Serie A was the pre-eminent national league and destination of choice for the world's best talent, hence Gascoigne signing for Lazio in 1992 and the demand for a weekly highlights package that attracted an audience of three million at its peak. The title was a play on the Gazza nickname (he was originally slated to present); lead presenter James Richardson also disclosed that the '*Golaccio*' cry was designed to sound like 'Go Lazio', though the Portuguese '*Golaço!*' actually means 'fantastic goal' and the credits deliberately mis-transcribed it. The title music was the work of Grammy-nominated songwriter and producer Steve DuBerry, who salvaged 'I'm Stronger Now', which he'd earlier released as half of Definitive Two (the other half being Ben Chapman) on the Deconstruction dance label. The '*Golaccio*' commentary sample came from dual-international José Altafini, who'd represented his native Brazil in the 1958 World Cup before becoming a naturalised Italian for 1962 and going on to commentate on Italian radio and TV. He was also part of the first wave of football pop stars, having released bossanova tune '*La Rosa*' while representing Napoli in 1967. And the same elongated goal celebration had already been sampled on Depth Charge's 'Goal' (1990).

The melody of '*Nessun Dorma*' is sampled in 'A Love So Beautiful' by American rock-balladeer Roy Orbison in collaboration with ELO's Jeff Lynne, first released in 1989 so narrowly beating the BBC to the punch. More rowdily, it was covered by heavy-metallers Manowar in 2002. It has also soundtracked films as disparate as *The Killing Fields* (1984), *Bend It Like Beckham* (2002) and *Mission: Impossible — Rogue Nation* (2015). Its sporting legacy is perhaps most clearly seen in English composer Tony Britten's UEFA Champions League Anthem. Though Britten was more heavily influenced by George Frideric Handel's 'Zadok the Priest', staff from International Sport and Leisure (ISL), a Swiss sports marketing company closely affiliated to FIFA, were so impressed by the BBC's concept that they took the same direction with their next project: rebranding the European Cup. Britten has said of his brief,

"The idea of Champions League was to make the game beautiful again, and the music had to reflect this quality." Job done, the verdict of Zinedine Zidane — a man who surely would have embellished Bernie's title sequence had it applied to any World Cup from France '98 onwards — sums up the transcendental qualities of both Puccini and Britten: "Magic ... it's magic above all else. When you hear [the music] it captivates you straight away."

Reviews

"The beautiful game was being played in a beautiful country famed for its classical arts and heritage and '*Nessun Dorma*' complemented Italy's staging of the World Cup perfectly."

– innovator Philip Bernie explains his radical choice in simple terms

"The phrases wash over you in waves. Then as it grows in passion, the tenor line becomes more declamatory with repeated notes as the orchestra swells poignantly underneath with bittersweet harmonic clashes in the counter melody. You sure know how to tug at our heart with your music, Giacomo."

– Classic FM

"It will be remembered as probably the outstanding theme of any major televised sporting event ever."

– BBC presenter Des Lynam

"Luciano is a born communicator. He only opens his mouth and with the first note, he gets the audience."

– one third of the Three Tenors, José Carreras

7. Three Lions

First released: 1996
Highest UK chart position: 1

Sonically, 'World in Motion' reigns supreme. But for its indelible impact and for encapsulating what it means to follow the England men's football team, 'Three Lions' is the de facto national anthem. As with other psalms to patriotism such as 'Rule, Britannia!', 'Three Lions' has found itself retrospectively denounced as imperialist. At the Russia 2018 World Cup, the perceived arrogance of its swelling chorus was cited as all the motivation needed by the Croatia camp to prolong England's disappointing tournament record. And co-author Frank Skinner felt moved to defend his work when Andy Anson, a major figure in England's failed bid to stage the 2018 World Cup, blamed the earlier failure of the 2006 bid on "an arrogant slogan": 'Football's coming home'.

'It's coming home' primarily referred to the sport returning to its roots, on the basis that the English Football Association were the first to formalise the rules in 1863. Who first kicked a ball, or a pig's bladder, or a sheep's, is open to dispute, and the very ratification of a shared pastime is open to accusations of colonialist administration. What was intended as a choral welcoming committee was also given a colonialist subtext by the fact that the one and only time an international tournament had previously been played in its fatherland, the patriarch had atypically emerged victorious. Therefore, the deeper England went in Euro '96 or any subsequent tournament, especially those played on foreign soil, that little pronoun 'it' acquired the weight of silverware instead. Triumphalism gathers momentum along with the melody.

In the poetry podcast that he has presented since 2020, Frank Skinner consistently avers that he is not a writer of verse. Yet if the beauty and brilliance of poetry lies in its being open to interpretation, then 'Three Lions' is up there with 'The Charge of the Light Brigade'. Its first words, spoken by Scotsman Alan Hansen, are "I think it's bad news for the English game", pointing us towards let-down. And that's not just the view of an outsider, to be scoffed at or thrown back in his face. It's followed by "We're not creative enough, and we're not positive enough", delivered by English gentleman Trevor Brooking. The criticism is fair and warranted. Yet this clear-spoken appraisal is undercut by the bed of restless crowd noises, the stirring of a rebellion, the common man rising up against the derisive voice of authority. The people still believe, even if the pundits don't. The tactic of utilising commentary had been used before in 'World in Motion' but, even with the disruptive background noise, the defeatist soundbites of 'Three Lions' set a very different tone to Kenneth Wolstenholme's chipper pronouncement. It might be coming home, but before anyone gets too carried away with the mounting tempo, Jimmy Hill chimes in with, "We'll go on getting bad results"! Even the more positive excerpts during the bridge — "England have done it, in the last minute of extra time!" (John Motson on David Platt's volley against Belgium in the round of 16, 1990) and "What a save, Gordon Banks!" (David Coleman on Banks's 'save of the century' in a group stage defeat to Brazil, 1970) — are delivered more in hope than expectation, and these chosen highlights are notably mediocre in the scheme of things.

Far from being a declaration of superiority, 'Three Lions' operates mostly as the antithesis of what an anthem should be, regaling us with its subject's deficiencies rather than strengths. Ironically, this is why it is cherished by the average football fan — the vast majority of club teams never win anything, silverware is always over the horizon, yet hope springs eternal and there is no question of supporters deserting. Stoically optimistic is the default mindset. For many, international football represents a better shot at a trophy than club football. Consequently, it would be perfectly understandable if the Three Lions' underachievements were a source of resentment, especially given the perpetual media cycle of hype, hysteria and censure. The genius of Skinner and David Baddiel was to counter the false confidence and to own the failure. Gallows humour is standard procedure at club level; in bringing it to the national conversation, contrary to the usual crowing about 'this time' and being 'the best', the comedians united supporters of all colours and rekindled affection towards the Saint George's Cross.

It probably helped that Skinner is a West Brom fan. Neutrals might be surprised to learn that the Baggies' years of hurt are actually two fewer than the Lions', having been FA Cup winners in 1968. Nevertheless, by 1996 they were a middling second-tier outfit, the obverse of glamour. Baddiel can be forgiven for being a Chelsea fan given that this was pre-Abramovich and the west Londoners had also been glory-free since 1971, bar the Zenith Data Systems Cup. Like Bernard Sumner before him, Ian Broudie of the Lightning Seeds (a Liverpudlian Red) recognised that there were people better qualified than him to lyrically bring the game to life. *Fantasy Football League* made Baddiel and Skinner the go-to lyricists for the blithe fans' perspective.

Broudie himself had been a staple of the Liverpool music scene since the late-Seventies, first as a member of Big in Japan and then as a producer for Echo and the Bunnymen, Shack and many more besides. The Lightning Seeds were a one-man band until Broudie created a touring ensemble to play the songs live in 1994. By this time, *Match of the Day* had begun using 'The Life of Riley', a minor Lightning Seeds hit from 1992, as the backing music to its Goal of the Month competition. This brought him to the attention of the FA, who asked Broudie to pen the official song for Euro '96. Football's homecoming was the obvious theme; it was apparently the FA's suggestion to refer to the Three Lions motif, which was lost on some contemporary journalists who had to ask what the trio of leos was in reference to. Recounting the making of the song, Broudie states:

> "I had the melody. It felt like a football song with a chorus that would make for a good chant. Liverpool were playing Leeds at Anfield midweek, so I invited Frank and David up to the studio. Frank came but David wasn't prepared to miss his beloved Chelsea, who were playing at home. After the match, I took Frank back to the studio, played him the idea on the piano, and we agreed we'd got something in the making."

Baddiel adds, "When we sat down to write, the first thing me and Frank talked about was reality: the reality of being an England fan that is. The show was about the reality of being a football fan and the way we approached the song was the same."

'Three Lions' is an example of what cultural theorist Mark Fisher dubbed 'ex-centric', in which English silliness acts as an antidote to imperial governance. Surrealism was writ large in *Fantasy Football League*, from Angus Loughran ('Statto') dispensing facts and figures in his pyjamas and dressing gown, to the 'Big Hello' (studio salutations to random dignitaries), to Jeff Astle Sings. The music video incorporated the homely setting of the TV show, designed to resemble the typical lad pad, with Broudie taking over the tea duties from Statto. Baddiel and Skinner in the Umbro '96 home shirt with the crest unusually centred (was merchandising behind its musical foregrounding?), Broudie wearing the iconic red '66 away shirt, the boys obey the typical matchday routine of heading to the pub, seemingly conforming to the stated purpose of the song: that is, representing the reality of being a fan. The obligatory football clips — a mixture of the great and not so great — are vindicated as diegetic viewing or edited in like memories from a photo album. The first hint of something truly illusory precedes the more upbeat commentary on the bridge, when hat-trick hero Geoff Hurst unassumingly works his way to the bar to pick up what appears to be a wine glass of H_2O. As the bridge fades into the refrain with the wistful lyric 'I know that was then but it could be again', we segue into the collective imagination and the football equivalent of Oz, where the everyday fan has a park kickabout with the professionals. This is where hope reaches its peak, representing what Baddiel termed 'magical thinking'.

This segment recreates the TV show's 'Phoenix from the Flames' bit, in which famous footballing moments are amateurishly reconstructed. Taking its cue from verse two, Stuart Pearce performs 'that tackle by Moore', Robbie Fowler plays Lineker scoring, Teddy Sheringham belts the ball like Bobby Charlton and Steve Stone dances a jig like Nobby Stiles, while the musician-fans fill in as supporting extras. Footballers have always held hero status but this silliness, this playfulness, this ordinariness humanises them in a way that was lost between the über-celebrity of David Beckham and Bukayo Saka's inflatable unicorn. A selection of players line up to sing the 'anthem' but Broudie tellingly didn't want them involved in the studio, not because of pitch or tuning concerns but in order to avoid the usual nationalistic trappings. Given their own vocal shortcomings, Baddiel and Skinner thought they were being cheeky in asking to sing as well as write, but the authentic voice is what was demanded. They therefore line up between the internationals, and the cross-cutting between park and pub reiterates that this is the people's anthem.

Incidentally, the players subsequently produced their own 'Phoenix from the Flames' moment, re-enacting the 'dentist's chair' after Gazza's wonder goal against Scotland. During a pre-tournament tour of Asia, pictures from an alcohol-fuelled night, in which players were reported to have been tied to a chair and plied with booze, found their way onto the front pages, with *The Sun* headline "DISGRACEFOOL" summing up the image of a worse-for-wear Gascoigne, Sheringham and Steve McManaman. After making a fool of Scotland captain Colin Hendry and beating Andy Goram, Gazza sprawls on his back and opens his mouth to be squirted with water by his obliging teammates. Just as 'Three Lions' sought to own the narrative, this was the players entertainingly reclaiming the narrative from the disparaging media. And after a lacklustre opening draw with Switzerland, it was also the precise moment at which the general public began to believe that there might be something special on the cards.

By this point, 'Three Lions' had already topped the charts, the only football song ever to enter at number one, indicative of the buzz around a home tournament but also the slicker promotional strategies that meant singles routinely peaked in their week of release in the mid-Nineties. It was usurped in its second week by another new entry, the Fugees' 'Killing Me Softly'. By contrast, the Beatles only ever had one song — 'Get Back' (1969) — go straight to the top; 'Free as a Bird', scraped together from an old John Lennon demo to publicise the *Anthology* series of releases, marked their second highest new entry in December 1995.

The mid-Nineties were a musical paradox; as well as heralding the modern drift towards instant gratification, they were also deeply nostalgic. The retro sounds and fashions of Britpop recycled the best of the Sixties and Seventies, with Oasis referencing the Beatles at every opportunity and Blur channelling the Kinks. The Lightning Seeds' melodic guitar pop fitted the Britpop mould, although Broudie's maturity and aloofness put them on the periphery of the movement. The sense of history repeating and the national pride engendered by Cool Britannia (a phrase ironically coined by the Bonzo Dog Doo-Dah Band's tongue-in-cheek take on 'Rule Britannia' from 1967) only intensified the belief that English football's time was coming again.

In the event, the boys of '96 couldn't quite emulate the boys of '66. Had Gazza's studs connected with Alan Shearer's ball across the face of goal in extra time of the semi-final, it could all have been a different story. As it was, England suffered a repeat of 1990 and penalty anguish at the feet of the Germans, leaving Euro '96 as another one of the 'oh-so-nears' aptly memorialised in its theme song. 'Three Lions' is about the English experience and so is unavoidably insular, yet it connected with the whole of Europe in the summer of '96, reaching number eight on the Eurochart Hot 100. It even made it to 49 on the Official German Charts and Jürgen Klinsmann, recently of Tottenham Hotspur, revealed that it had been sung on the German team bus; it was also sung by the crowd when the trophy was paraded on the Römer balcony in Frankfurt, so the triumphalism associated with the song emanates from Germany as much as anywhere else. It also returned to number one in the UK chart the week after the final, a success attributable either to a disproportionate number of German expats among the record-buying public or, more likely, England fans wallowing in the predicted heartbreak.

Never ones to stop dreaming, England supporters returned 'Three Lions' (re-recorded as '3 Lions '98') to the top of the charts during the France 1998 World Cup. 'Jules Rimet still gleaming' had been declared an anachronism by some commentators given that it wasn't up for grabs at the European Championships. Nor was it the prize at the '98 World Cup, having been retired to Brazil when their third tournament conquest in 1970 entitled them to keep the trophy in perpetuity (it was subsequently stolen in 1983). This interpretation, though, repeats the misreading of the song as triumphalist: the trophy was not a target but a rose-tinted memory.

Two years on, Euro '96 was a bittersweet memory. The clamour that begins '3 Lions '98' is a terrace hollering of 'It's coming home' and Jonathan Pearce's commentary outtake alludes to the festival atmosphere. Meanwhile, in the updated video, Baddiel, Skinner and Broudie congregate in the pouring rain to watch Gareth Southgate's fateful penalty miss through the window of an electronics shop, very much the outsiders but buoyed by the new refrain — making explicit what was implicit in the original — 'We still believe'. The remembered glories of the second verse have given way to:

And now I see Ince ready for war

[*the midfield general bandaged up in a pivotal World Cup qualifier in hostile Roman territory*]

Gazza good as before

[*lighting up a second tournament somewhat against the odds in the wake of serious injury*]

Shearer certain to score

[*five goals earned the reliable centre-forward the Golden Boot award at Euro '96*]

And Psycho screaming ...

[*Stuart Pearce's reaction after slaying the demons of his Italia '90 penalty miss with a smashed conversion in Euro '96's quarter-final against Spain*]

The first image was a cannibalisation of 'Butcher ready for war', which referred to famously bloodied centre-back Terry Butcher in a 1989 WC qualifier in Sweden. This line had to be replaced in the original edit by 'Bobby belting the ball' owing to the FA's ongoing squeamishness around violent imagery. Come 1998, it wasn't the official song and censorship could be disregarded. Official duties passed to England United, bizarrely comprised of Ian McCulloch (Echo and the Bunnymen), Johnny Marr (The Smiths), Simon Fowler (Ocean Colour Scene), Tommy Scott (Space) and the Spice Girls (their last recording before Geri Halliwell's departure). The result was '(How Does It Feel To Be) On Top of the World', which was a half-proud, half-apologetic mish-mash that stalled at number nine and got booed when played at a Wembley warm-up.

Back to the '3 Lions '98' video and our triumvirate are joined on the sojourn to France by an army of travelling fans, apropos to the camaraderie that the song instilled. And when they encounter a coachload of German 'Kuntz' (a predictably cheeky shirt reference to striker Stefan) it all kicks off in the car park with an impromptu jumpers for goalposts friendly that recalls the Christmas truce of 1914. Again, apropos to the song, the ball might have belonged to England, they might have started the game, but it's a global affair that they have no God-given right to win. The lyrics may have changed but the sentiment hadn't.

'Three Lions' actually shares the dubious honour of being one of three songs to have reached number one with different sets of lyrics. The other two? 'Do They Know It's Christmas?' (Band Aid, Band Aid II, Band Aid 20 and Band Aid 30) and 'Mambo No. 5' (Lou Bega and Bob the Builder). It is also a record holder for most separate stints at number one: two non-consecutive weeks in 1996, the reissue in 1998, and again on the strength of streaming and England's surge to another semi-final in 2018, when defeat to Croatia triggered an unwanted record of the sharpest ever descent from the number one spot (all the way down to 97).

The song resurfaces in one form or another at every major tournament England attend. During the women's European Championships in 2022, it somehow failed to dent the charts, despite the Lionesses bringing an end to all those years of hurt. Between semi-final and final, however, it did receive another rewrite, with singer-songwriter-footballer Chelcee Grimes standing in for Frank Skinner at a National Lottery-hosted gig at Camden's Electric Ballroom. Grimes, who has written for Kylie Minogue and Dua Lipa and played for Everton and Tottenham, joined Broudie and Baddiel on stage to eulogise 'Ellen White standing tall' and 'Russo ready to score'. It wasn't Alessia Russo but fellow substitute Chloe Kelly who scored the winner against nemeses Germany, precipitating a more fêted rendition, when the champions raucously gatecrashed manager Sarina Wiegman's post-match press conference and danced on the tables to the jubilant refrain of 'It's coming home'.

Baddiel remarked that this might be the opportune time to 'put [the song] to bed' but it was instead remade into '56 years of hurt for the men's game ... 20 weeks of hurt for the women's game' in 'Three Lions (It's Coming Home for Christmas)', released for the unseasonal Qatar World Cup. Beginning with the chanting Lionesses mingled with sleigh bells, the video cuts to reveal a youthful Baddiel and Skinner watching Leah Williamson's conga line on their tiny Nineties TV. A latter-day Broudie is superimposed next to his younger self in the original video before it pans to the latter-day Baddiel and Skinner entering through the front door, marking a transition to the Christmas-themed present. Full of self-deprecation, the creators said they couldn't resist having 'one more go for the blokes', and it's worth it just for Geoff Hurst dressed as Santa completing a hat-trick of video cameos.

Even if that is the instigators done with it, it's harder to envisage a time when excitable England supporters won't sing 'Three Lions' than it is to envisage the England men's team finally providing justification for the triumphalism it incites. As the Three Lions reached their first final on international soil at Euro 2024, the song that popularised that moniker again breached the UK top 10, though as the years of hurt stretch interminably on, folk are becoming more circumspect. On the eve of the match against Spain, Gary Lineker was asked by his BBC paymasters if football was coming home. "I'm banning that statement," he replied. "It's been bad luck for so long."

Reviews

"The song is humour isn't it — it is English humour. Unless you're a fan of *Fawlty Towers* and stuff like that maybe you don't get the slant on it."

– England manager Gareth Southgate having his say in 2018

"Basically no one knew the song had taken root at that point. At the end of the game the DJ put the song on and 87,000 people joined in spontaneously, which is an extraordinary thing to happen. You're supposed to say the best day of your life is when your children are born — I'm not so sure of that."

– David Baddiel on England 2-0 Scotland, 15 June 1996

"A real key-tapper."

– the verdict of contemporary England manager Terry Venables bemused Baddiel and Skinner

"It's no classic, and may not figure too highly in critics' end-of-year polls, but as a traditional football anthem it does the job of appealing to eight-year-olds and the man on the Wembley omnibus alike."

– Johnny Cigarettes and Steve Sutherland, *NME*

"As football songs go, 'Three Lions' is certainly the best."

– astute commentator John Motson

8. Together Stronger (C'mon Wales)

First released: 2016
Highest UK chart position: N/A

The Welsh have a proud choral tradition. Nicknamed the Land of Song (among other things), the cultural significance of music and poetry can be traced back to its Celtic roots, and the consonantal nature of the Welsh language is innately melodic according to students of linguistics. John Ford's *How Green Was My Valley*, which beat *Citizen Kane* to Outstanding Motion Picture at the 1942 Academy Awards, transported Maureen O'Hara to a Welsh mining village and contained the line, adapted from Richard Llewellyn's source novel, "Singing is in my people as sight is in the eye." A tradition of congregational singing was strengthened in the collieries as new communities sprung up around the expanding coal and iron industries in the 18th and 19th centuries; according to Gareth Williams, Emeritus History Professor at the University of South Wales: "In unfamiliar new surroundings [men] found solace and sociability in song, for in a materially poor society the voice was the most democratic of instruments; it cost nothing, for most of us have a voice."

What the Welsh don't have is a proud tradition of reaching association football's major championships. While 'Three Lions' bemoaned 30 years of hurt since being the last ones standing at an international festival of football, by the time Wales reached Euro 2016 their supporters had spent 58 years simply waiting for the chance to get the party started. Their appearance at the 1958 World Cup in Sweden predates all our international hits and was most notable for witnessing Pelé's first World Cup goal, which knocked the Welsh out at the quarter-final stage. Their last outright victory in the Home International Championship dates back to 1952, with the singing tradition largely revolving around the oval ball game instead.

On a side note, there was at least some Welsh interest in what football writer Henry Winter has referred to as "the decade when football went pop" (in a review of Jon Spurling's *Get It On: How the '70s Rocked Football*). Amongst the explosion of personalities was Giorgio Chinaglio. The Welsh-Italian connection of Pavarotti's big break at the 1955 Eisteddfod is reaffirmed in the colourful story of Chinaglio, whose family moved from Tuscany to Cardiff that same year since his father was a steelworker in search of employment. Aged eight at the time, he picked up a Welsh accent at school and began his professional career with Swansea City. He was released by the third division club in 1966 after only six appearances — but eight years later, he was firing Lazio to their first Scudetto. At the height of his fame and popularity in Italy, he released the English-language song '(I'm) Football Crazy' on RCA Records:

Sunday morn', rain or shine
Gotta make the game on time
All week long, gotta train
Cos I'm better than the rest!

The professionalism attributed to him by songwriters Guido and Maurizio De Angelis was a tad misplaced. The narcissism, on the other hand, fits to a tee. At the 1974 World Cup, he insulted the Italian coaching staff and smashed up the dressing room after being substituted against Haiti. In 1976, he turned his back on Italy and joined the influx of stars to the North American Soccer League, of which Phil Woosnam (cousin of golfer Ian and a footballer for Wales, Leyton Orient, West Ham United, Aston Villa and Atlanta Chiefs) had been a founding figure. The Kairdiff Kid (his pronunciation) outgunned Pelé at the New York Cosmos (193 goals in 213 appearances) and counted Frank Sinatra and Mick Jagger as associates. He returned to Lazio as club president in 1983, but nearly bankrupted them, and had to serve an eight-month suspension for attacking a referee with an umbrella. He spent his final days in Florida, exiled from Italy, where a warrant had been issued for his arrest over allegations of money-laundering and an attempted Mafia takeover of Lazio which he had fronted.

Chinaglio is the kind of extrovert character the Manic Street Preachers might have written about. Marrying a glam-punk attitude with socialist ideals, the Manics of *Generation Terrorists* (1992) wouldn't have been obvious contenders to helm an anthem of national unity, yet their oeuvre always contained strong traces of Welsh national pride. Their mainstream breakthrough, 'A Design for Life', was heavily indebted to Joy Division's *An Ideal for Living* EP but its assertive opening line ('Libraries gave us power') also drew from a legend engraved above the entrance to the former library in Pillgwenlly, Newport, close to the band's hometown of Blackwood, which read "Knowledge is Power". And the title of their first number one album, *This Is My Truth Tell Me Yours* (1998), quotes Welsh politician Aneurin Bevan, MP for Ebbw Vale from 1928 to 1960 and widely credited as the founder of the NHS.

They were also leading figures of Cŵl Cymru (Cool Wales), a cultural movement to rival Cool Britannia that coincided with Welsh devolution and the formation of the National Assembly. Journalist Iain Ellis posits that if Britpop was a reaction to grunge and American cultural imperialism, for Welsh bands the enemy was not America but England — "the enemy within". The Land of Song possessed "a largely barren rock history" and was characterised instead by crooners such as Tom Jones and Shirley Bassey, while mavericks such as John Cale fled the nest at the earliest opportunity. This meant that while Menswear, Ocean Colour Scene and Cast bathed in the refracted glory of the Who, the Yardbirds and the Animals, the Welsh felt little affinity with the scene. The movers and shakers of Cŵl Cymru were partly subsumed by Cool Britannia but generally fell into two camps: English-language bands with international ambitions beyond the narrow borders of Britpop (Manic Street Preachers, Stereophonics) and more self-consciously Welsh acts (Super Furry Animals, Gorky's Zygotic Mynci, Catatonia).

'Together Stronger' sounds much more like a unionist slogan than a separatist one, even with the 'C'mon Wales' appendage, and might have served as an effective slogan for the Remain campaign in the Brexit referendum, which clashed with Euro 2016 and at which the majority of Wales, along with the rest of the UK, voted to leave the EU at the exact same time the Red Dragons were returning to the continental stage. The international outlook of the Manics was therefore well suited to a gathering across the channel that Welsh fans were ecstatic just to be a part of.

All members of the Manic Street Preachers were born at the tail-end of the Swinging Sixties, more than a decade after Wales' last bow at an international tournament. They had therefore grown up suffering the slings and arrows of perennial qualifying failures. As per 'Three Lions', the standouts are referenced in the lyrics:

> Joe Jordan won with his hand
> [*the striker's transgression helped send Scotland to the 1978 World Cup at Wales' expense*]
> Russia was Giggsy's last chance
> [*the lost 2004 European Championship play-off*]
> Paul Bodin's penalty miss
> [*the width of a crossbar away from a place at USA 1994*]
> That '85 night was so tragic'
> [*Scotland again secured World Cup qualification at Wales' expense but the real tragedy was the collapse and death of victorious manager Jock Stein*]

Just as Stein's death put football sorrows into perspective, Wales' newfound success was tempered by the absence of Gary Speed, who'd shockingly died by suicide while in post as Wales manager in 2011. The Manics were themselves personally acquainted with tragedy; fourth founding member Richey Edwards was missing presumed dead since 1995, so 'Let's not forget Gary Speed' carried extra resonance when sung by James Dean Bradfield.

Heartfelt as 'Together Stronger' is though, it's not exactly 'Roses in the Hospital'. The profusion of football song tropes gives the sense that the lyrics could have been phoned in. The end of the second verse — 'You're just too good to be true / We can't take our eyes off you' — is particularly revealing; the song was initially conceived as a reworking of the 1967 Frankie Valli hit which had become a favourite in Welsh football's repertoire. 'Can't Take My Eyes Off You' is sung with gusto at various grounds such as Fulham's Craven Cottage; its connection to Wales dates back to 1993 and a BBC promotional campaign. John Morgan, head of presentation and promos for BBC Wales, was putting together a short film for the pivotal World Cup qualifier against Romania at Cardiff Arms Park. It occurred to him that the most popular chant of the time — 'All we are singing, is give us a goal' to the tune of John Lennon's 'Give Peace a Chance' — was more desperate than inspirational, so he recorded himself and his production team singing the more uplifting Valli tune, which was then edited over action footage of contemporary Welsh heroes such as Ian Rush, Ryan Giggs and Gary Speed. Played multiple times before kick-off, it caught on, as Morgan intended. A Manic Street Preachers' cover version appears on the rarities album *Lipstick Traces* (2003) and Bradfield performed an acoustic version to ring in midnight at the band's 1999 New Year's Eve concert at Cardiff's Millennium Stadium. The Stereophonics' Kelly Jones also recorded an acoustic version which was played in tribute to Speed at the cherished Welshman's funeral. The intricacies of music licensing meant that, despite its ongoing association with the Welsh national team, its publishers refused permission for 'Can't Take My Eyes Off

You' to be officially released and so the Manics hastily assembled their own stadium rock backing track.

The sleeve art walks the same tightrope as the recording, balancing past and present, merriment and respect, parochialism and universality. It depicts the band, star players Gareth Bale, Aaron Ramsey and Ashley Williams, and Speed's successor Chris Coleman in V-formation, Bradfield at the tip wielding his guitar — emblazoned with the Welsh dragon emblem — as if it were a sword. The flag hovers behind, fading into the impressive Welsh mountains, and the overall layout and colour scheme is dictated by the national banner.

In view of the team's unparalleled success in reaching the semi-finals, combined with the Manics' previous chart success, the failure of 'Together Stronger' to breach the UK singles top 100 is an enigma to rival Lonnie Donegan and 'World Cup Willie'. In terms of physical sales, it was the principality's best-seller, CD copies no doubt proving popular souvenirs for the generations of Welsh football fans who'd been waiting since the early days of Elvis for an anthem of their own. This also makes it a perfect case study in the vagaries of the UK chart in an era of streams and downloads, when declining physical sales are dwarfed by digital consumption and online charts are updated daily, combining with the corrosion of industry-standard release patterns to make rankings more susceptible to manipulation. Even the donation of all profits to the Princes Gate Trust and Tenovus Cancer Care couldn't garner the clicks needed to register with the Official Charts Company.

If the official anthem by the Manic Street Preachers failed to chart, then what chance did the unofficial anthem by the Super Furry Animals have?! Euro 2016 brought the Britpop outliers back into the studio for the first time in seven years, inspired by the rise of Chris Coleman's boys to dust off a demo prepared in hope for the 2004 Euros. 'Bing Bong' is a gloriously bonkers slice of Welsh Krautrock which frontman Gruff Rhys explains thus:

"'Bing Bong' is a Welsh folk idiom that we have appropriated, but its pronunciation has been partly inspired by the sonic motif of the talking robot, Twiki, in the 1979-81 sci-fi series *Buck Rodgers in the 25th Century.*"

Okaaay ... The song's twitching bassline and heavily vocoded vocals were aired at Swansea's Liberty Stadium on the opening date of the band's 20th anniversary tour, shortly before Euro 2016 kicked off. They then detoured to Toulouse to play a specially arranged gig the night before Wales' first ever European Championship Finals match. The army tank that they had modified into a sound system and driven to festivals in the Nineties was by now decommissioned, which was probably for the best. The Super Furries are so singularly offbeat that half of the time it's difficult to tell if Rhys is singing in English or Welsh; 'Bing Bong' follows their Welsh-language album *Mwng* (2000) in upholding what had been a minority language since the 1911 Census revealed that only 43.5% of the population spoke Cymraeg. By 2011 that figure had dwindled to 19%.

The revival of the Welsh language has been a pressing social, political and cultural concern since the mid-20th century. In the 1970s, folk singer Dafydd Iwan was briefly imprisoned for defacing English road signs in Carmarthenshire. In the early-1980s, he wrote 'Yma o Hyd' (Still Here), which lauds the survival of the Welsh identity 'despite everyone and everything'. 'Ry'n ni yma o hyd' (We're still here) is repeated 19 times across the song's four-and-a-half minutes. It would have been a fitting football anthem any time between 1958 and 2016. Using a Welsh-language song to announce Wales' revival was practically inconceivable in 2016 however. The run to the semi-finals, led by the talismanic Bale — who would later upset his La Liga paymasters by holding aloft a flag stating "Wales. Golf. Madrid. In that order" — provoked a sea change in the national psyche. Rugby union is widely considered the national sport of Wales but its global influence is negligible; to hold their own in the world's favourite sport was an enormous boon to their cultural wellbeing. And with that, the revival of 'Yma o Hyd' commenced.

The song had been a mainstay of pre-match preparations at Wales Women football matches, at Wrexham AFC and at the rugby for some time. Iwan, whose singing career had been placed on hold during his tenure as president of Plaid Cymru from 2003 to 2010, was invited to perform at the Cardiff City Stadium before the crucial 2022 World Cup play-off games against Austria and Ukraine. Its burgeoning popularity saw it reach the top of the iTunes chart three days after Bale's free kick booked Wales a ticket to their first World Cup in 64 years, at which 'Yma o Hyd' was the Red Wall's approved anthem. Welsh drill artist Sage Todz also recorded a more cutting-edge version, 'O HYD', supported by the Football Association of Wales. Head of Content and Engagement, Rob Dowling said:

> "The FAW is a modern, progressive organisation that doesn't need to play by the conventional rules of others. We naturally engage with modern Welsh culture to highlight not only the talent within the country, but also to represent the diversity of that culture, where people express their national identity in many different forms."

Together stronger. Or gyda'n gilydd yn gryfach.

Reviews

"It was a proper bucket-list moment, y'know. So many times over the last 20 years I've started to write a lyric when we've been in a play-off or close to qualifying and to actually be able to do it and for the FAW to ask us to do the official one, dream come true."

– Manics bassist and lyricist Nicky Wire speaking to BBC Wales News

"It was rockin'. Everyone had to get involved and it was something new to us but we all enjoyed it and it's a great song."

– midfielder Joe Ledley

"It was fantastic to be involved with such an iconic Welsh band."

– manager Chris Coleman

"You always wonder if you can actually pull off a football song, because let's face it there have been so many bad ones out there. We've got to admit that the benchmarks are 'Three Lions' and 'World in Motion' — they are two great football songs. I thought we had a good chance because I knew that Nick would write such a well-informed lyric — there would be so much history in there."

– James Dean Bradfield

"The stirring string-laden anthem is sure to send shivers racing down the spine of any self-respecting Welsh football fan."

– David Owens, Wales Online

9. Far Away in America

First released: 1994
Highest UK chart position: N/A

'Two World Wars and one World Cup
England, England'

The boorish mentality of this half-a-century-old chant, set to the tune of American minstrel song 'Camptown Races', does a disservice to the lyricism of English songwriting. Ignoring the fact that it's more difficult to fit four World Cups, three European Championships and a superior economy to a melody, Germany have little reason to be cowed by our footballing and military might, but they are rightfully envious of our music industry. And even though Die Deutsche Fußballnationalmannschaft sounds like it could be a Kraftwerk album, Ralf and Florian are more into the Tour de France than the Bundesliga.

Despite the historical enmity between England and Germany, the two nations have much in common and sporting singalongs are a shared passion, hence Klinsmann and the gang appropriating the refrain from 'Three Lions'. In 2012, the legendary Franz Beckenbauer chastised the players for not showing sufficient passion in the singing of national anthem '*Das Deutschlandlied*' before their defeat to Italy at the semi-final stage of the European Championships. He stated afterwards, "Ardour must begin before kick-off and singing loudly together helps with that."

'Der Kaiser' knew a thing or two about group bonding, having captained West Germany to victory at the 1972 European Championship and the 1974 World Cup, while in between leading them in song for '*Fußball ist unser Leben*' (Football Is Our Life). This was the national team's debut recording, but giddy with success and the joy of hosting the forthcoming World Cup, and perhaps inspired by England's 'Cinnamon Stick', they also produced an album of the same name, which serves as a totem of Schlager, a distinctly German genre of modern light music. It was composed and produced by Jack White — not the embryonic White Stripe, but Horst Nußbaum, who played for Cologne and PSV Eindhoven before embarking on a recording career that also saw him join forces with Engelbert Humperdinck, Tony Christie and David Hasselhoff under the anglicised pseudonym that exhibits the Anglo-American dominance of the industry. Always one to lead by example, Beckenbauer had issued a solo single in 1967, '*Gute Freunde Kann Niemand Trennen*' (Nobody Can Separate Good Friends), which reached number 31 in the German charts and is basically an audition for a Bing Crosby version of *Escape to Victory*. '*Fußball ist unser Leben*' peaked at number 27. Remixed for 2006, when Germany next hosted the World Cup, it bombed at 71.

The most commercially successful German football song is '*Buenos Dias Argentina*' from 1978, which was a number 3 hit and was again accompanied by an LP of the same name which knocked Buddy Holly's *Greatest Hits* off the top of the album charts and obtained platinum status. The guiding creative force on this occasion was Udo Jürgens, who had triumphed at the 1966 Eurovision Song Contest for Austria (Germany's maiden win came in 1982, in Harrogate of all places, with '*Ein bißchen Frieden*' by Nicole, written by Ralph Siegel and Bernd Meinunger — more on them in a moment). In an inauspicious twist of fate, it was Jürgens' native Austria who knocked Germany out in Argentina '78 by defeating them 3-2 in the second group stage. Nonetheless, *Buenos Dias Argentina* exemplifies both the German penchant for a long player and their gracious global outlook, paying compliment to the host country of the World Cup. It was followed by albums titled *Olé España* (1982, another number one), *Mexico Mi Amor* (1986) and *Sempre Roma* (which reunited *Die Deutsche Fußballnationalmannschaft* with Udo Jürgens in 1990).

Something special was required for the next in the sequence. In 1994, Germany were reigning champions. It was also the first World Cup since 1938 as a unified Germany; East Germany's relative lack of success means that the West are regarded as the de facto *Fußballnationalmannschaft*, and though Euro '92 marked the first international tournament since the fall of the Berlin Wall, for some reason the Germans have never seen fit to commemorate European Championships with singles or albums. Last but by no means least, the 1994 World Cup was taking place in the home of modern music, the country that had gifted the world Motown, Philly soul and disco.

Coming out of New York's disco scene and making it big in Germany, and indeed most of the world, were the Village People. The group's name refers to New York's Greenwich Village, a famously counter-cultural neighbourhood on the Lower East Side of Manhattan. It was also the site of the 1969 Stonewall Riots, which gave rise to the gay liberation movement. The Village People were the front for French producers Jacques Morali (homosexual) and Henri Belolo (heterosexual), who targeted disco's sizeable gay audience with a group made up of macho gay-fantasy personas. Morali sadly died of AIDS-related causes in 1991, while the Village People hadn't enjoyed a top ten hit anywhere since 1980, though 1985's 'Sex Over the Phone' performed better in Germany than anywhere else (number 40). Enter music mogul Ralph Siegel, who thought it a good idea to add 'soccer player' to the cop/Native American/GI/sailor/

construction worker/cowboy/biker (also known as 'leatherman') line-up.

Siegel was the writer/producer behind Germany's 1982 and 1986 recordings. He also participated in the Eurovision Song Contest on a whopping 24 occasions, writing entries for Germany, Luxembourg, Switzerland, Montenegro and San Marino, mostly in tandem with lyricist Bernd Meinunger, who was entrusted with penning the words to 'Far Away in America'. As magnificent as the collective handle Die Deutsche Fußballnationalmannschaft and the Village People may be, appealing to both camps was an undeniably tricky task. While making no explicit reference to sport but implying competition and camaraderie, Meinunger also piled up sexual double entendres, such as 'get it out and shake it' and 'touching you deep inside'. Even in the modern age of the Rainbow Laces campaign by LGBTQ+ charity Stonewall (named after the instrumental Greenwich Village bar), football culture isn't entirely at ease with homosexuality, so it's no great surprise that virulently masculine Nineties footballers appeared uncomfortable bopping along to the lyric 'there's a rainbow in your eyes'. The atmosphere in the recording studio was purportedly frosty, although Jürgen Klinsmann — perhaps in preparation for the international statesman role awaiting him as manager of both Germany and the United States — smiles diplomatically and musters more enthusiasm than most in the accompanying music video.

The public weren't sure what to make of this bizarre collaboration either. The British are often accused of living off historical conquests; a modern unified Germany had less call for living in the past but singing in English alongside a group of homosexuals still sat uncomfortably with a resurgent nation only a couple of generations removed from the Nazi ideology of the master race. 'Far Away in America' only reached number 44 in the German charts and did nothing to revitalise the career of the Village People. Californian band Weezer might have made happier teammates; frontman Rivers Cuomo is a noted soccer enthusiast who provided unofficial anthems for the US men's team in 2006 ('My Day is Coming') and 2010

('Represent'). Fresh off catchy breakout hit 'Buddy Holly' in 1994, it would have neatly joined the dots with *Buenos Dias Argentina*, which had knocked the bespectacled Buddy from the top of the album charts all those years before. Evidently, South America fared better in Germany than North.

'Faraway in America' signalled the end of *Die Deutsche Fußballnationalmannschaft*'s recording career, at least for the time being. Still, it wasn't the biggest musical misfire of USA '94. That honour belongs to soul diva Diana Ross's epic fail from the penalty spot during the opening ceremony. She was singing gay anthem 'I'm Coming Out' at the time. There is a distinct possibility that, between them, Ross and the Village People set men's soccer's acceptance of the gay community back by a whole generation — German international Thomas Hitzlsperger (who also represented Aston Villa, VfB Stuttgart and Lazio at club level) is the most high-profile footballer to date to come out and he didn't feel comfortable doing so until a year after calling time on his career; he was a 12-year-old on the books of Bayern Munich when senior pros Oliver Kahn, Thomas Helmer and Lothar Matthäus were awkward partners with Greenwich Village's finest. At the 2022 Qatar World Cup, with LGBTQ+ 'One Love' armbands prohibited by the host country, in which same-sex relationships are criminalised, and FIFA regressively threatening sanctions against any wearers, the German team staged a silent protest by symbolically covering their mouths during the pre-match formalities. A statement from the German FA declared, "Denying us the armband is the same as denying us a voice ... It wasn't about making a political statement — human rights are non-negotiable." Unfortunately, the chances for further protest were limited as they exited at the group stage, with nationalistic critics arguing that they should have concentrated more on football and less on social issues.

Protest songs reverberate around the stands but are a rarely visited subgenre of the recorded football anthem; had *Die Deutsche Fußballnationalmannschaft* allied with the Village People in 2022, the results could have been very different.

Reviews

"Watching soccer players appear in music videos is a unique study in terror. These are athletes at the top of their game, usually so confident and assured. But as soon as that camera rolls a cardboard-like stiffness sets in, all the face muscles tense up, and the only movement they're capable of is a rigid side-to-side shuffle. Look closely, though, and you'll see an exception to the rule here: Jürgen Klinsmann and his tousled blonde locks, bouncing away in a carefree manner, seemingly at ease with this whole 'America' thing and perhaps even inspired by the Village People's clunky nationalist browbeating."

– Nick Neyland, Pitchfork

"Catchy, camp and anthemic, 'Far Away in America' is vintage stuff from the band who ruled the world with 'YMCA' in the disco era, but it was sadly stiff-armed by the record buying public in Germany."

– Jeremy Allen, BBC Music

"For sheer entertainment value, in the 'what were they thinking?' variety, few World Cup songs can match this delight."

– Scott Roxborough, *The Hollywood Reporter*

"On one occasion, we were in the away dressing room and the opposition knocked our door down. They sang Buju Banton's 'Boom Bye Bye'; a song about shooting 'queers', that they all need to be dead. For a few weeks, I lost my love of football. Today, we actually have trouble recruiting for Stonewall FC. At 'straight' clubs, player's mates don't care if they're gay anymore, so why would they need to join us? In our first-team, there are five straight players. It's because they're here for the football, no one discriminates. They feel totally comfortable and we feel comfortable with them. Things have changed massively."

– Aslie Pitter MBE, who co-founded Stonewall FC in 1991

10. Rise Up

First released: 1998
Highest UK chart position: 54

The United Kingdom and the United States might be the prime exporters of pop culture, but one Caribbean island is so concomitant with a particular genre that its men's national soccer team are known as the Reggae Boyz. Thank heavens that the Reggae Boyz eventually made it to a World Cup so that the Reggae All-Starz, aka Jamaica United, could assemble in celebration.

Jamaica's greatest musical export, Bob Marley, never wrote a football song, although the beatific 'Three Little Birds' fluttered into the hearts of Ajax supporters via a pre-season friendly at Ninian Park in 2008. An ephemeral moment that somehow became embedded in the club's DNA, stadium announcer Ali Yassine pressed play on Bob Marley and the Wailers' positive vibes in order to placate the away supporters who were being kept behind in the stadium while Cardiff City supporters dispersed. The Amsterdam contingent gleefully grooved along and carried the vibes all the way back to the Johan Cruyff Arena where, 10 years later, Marley's son Ky-Mani

Marley would lead them in a half-time singalong. In 2021, on the 40th anniversary of Bob Marley's death, Ajax produced a special 'Three Little Birds' third kit, which the club marketing manager claimed "sold at least four times more than any other Ajax shirt" but couldn't be used competitively because it fell foul of UEFA's regulation forbidding different forms of identification other than the club and sponsor logos.

Marley himself loved football. He was a skilful dribbler who equated football with freedom and saw it as another form of artistic expression, albeit a less peaceful one. He once told a journalist, "If you want to get to know me, you will have to play football against me and the Wailers", and in an interview in 1980 he said, "I love music before I love football. If I [play] football first it maybe can be dangerous. I sing about peace, love and all that stuff, and something might happen y'know. If a man tackle you hard it bring feelings of war." His daughter Cedella Marley intervened to save the women's national team, the Reggae Girlz, from being wound up in 2014 and told BBC Sport that her father would have been proud: "He'd be like, 'that's my girl'."

Cedella also performed with her siblings as the Melody Makers, named after the UK music weekly, and fronted by Bob's eldest child, Ziggy. Christened David Nesta Marley, the origin of the Ziggy sobriquet is disputed; some reports state that it is a slang term meaning 'little spliff' and was a term of endearment used by his father, while Ziggy himself told *Melody Maker* in 1988, "Me name David but me big Bowie fan. So at the time of the Ziggy Stardust album, me call meself Ziggy and now everyone do."

Ziggy Marley and the Melody Makers' debut recording came as early as 1979, with 'Children Playing in the Streets', written by Bob in aid of the United Nations' International Year of the Child. The lyrics are sadly more concerned with child poverty and ghetto life than jumpers for goalposts and next goal wins. The Melody Makers' debut album was *Play the Game Right* (1985, again about the metaphorical game of life rather than a clampdown on diving and time-wasting) and they remained active until 2002. Ziggy then embarked on a solo career, but had already recorded sans siblings as the driving force behind Jamaica United.

Cricket might be the national sport, and Usain Bolt has since inspired youngsters to slip on running spikes rather than football boots, but the world's fastest man dreamt of playing for Manchester United and football is in the blood of many Jamaicans. It was therefore carnival time when the Reggae Boyz qualified for their first World Cup in 1998. Jamaica United, sounding like the club edition of the national side, recruited reggae and dancehall royalty to sing in praise of this achievement. As well as Ziggy Marley, who was principal songwriter on 'Rise Up', the singing team consisted of Frederick 'Toots' Hibbert (of rocksteady legends Toots and the Maytals), Shaggy (of 'Oh Carolina', 'Boombastic' and 'It Wasn't Me' fame), Maxi Priest ('Wild World', 'Close to You'), Ini Kamoze ('Here Comes the Hotstepper'), Diana King ('Shy Guy'), Buju Banton (probably best known in the UK for controversies surrounding homophobic lyrics and drug charges), Brian Gold, Richie Stephens, Tony Rebel and Bob Marley's back-up singers the I-Threes. On the production team were Sly Dunbar (one half of the prolific rhythm section and production duo Sly and Robbie, who had already undertaken a recording session with the Reggae Boyz, the result of which was the overlooked 'Kick It'), the Beatmasters (responsible for multiple smash hits, including Betty Boo's 'Doin' the Doo' and Aswad's 'Shine'), James Reynolds, Mikey Bennett and Handel Tucker.

The essence of the song is there in the title and is familiar from classic reggae: mysticism merged with social mobility and zeal ...

> The expectation of a nation's like music to the ear
> Oooooo we're singing a brand new song
> Marching to a brand new beat
> Down the inside, through the palace, filling every street

Like a ragga pick and mix, each artist brings a dash of their own unique style, which can be a bit reductive, especially King's vignette, which is little more than a reprisal of the lyrical hook from 'Shy Guy' (a 1995 hit from the *Bad Boys* movie starring Will Smith), although her voice still stands out as the first female one in this entire compilation of football recordings.

The Reggae Boyz were unsurprisingly knocked out at the group stages, but performed respectably and, by beating Japan, achieved the Caribbean's first World Cup Finals victory since Cuba in 1938. 'Rise Up' was the soundtrack to their short-lived moment in the sun, although the scale of its success is difficult to ascertain since the Jamaica Music Countdown was only introduced in 2007. In the UK, it failed to breach the top 40, which is surprising given the size of the West Indian diaspora, the contributing artists' popularity (10 top 20 hits in the preceding five years) and the relative quality of Jamaica United and England United.

The striking similarity in the national supergroups' names is symptomatic of the shared customs and the post-war cultural exchange initiated by the Windrush Generation; Jamaica gave us John Barnes and Bob Marley, we reciprocated with Robbie Earle and UB40. A Channel 4 documentary on the eve of France '98 highlighted the disparity in the lifestyles of the English Premier League players and those who played in the Jamaica National Premier League for the likes of Violet Kickers and Harbour View, which was later said to have damaged the harmony of the group. Earle disputes this:

> "Nothing was further from the truth. To be honest, some of the guys who played in Jamaica were more professional than some pros I played with and who were getting paid thousands of pounds per week. The camp was very different. Basically, it was a glorified club team but in the guise of a national team."

Jokingly, the Reggae Boyz' British-born players such as Earle, Fitzroy Simpson, Marcus Gayle, Deon Burton, Frank Sinclair and Paul Hall were dubbed the UB40s in reference to the Birmingham pop-reggae act. The Black Country's partiality towards reggae can also be heard in West Bromwich Albion and Wolverhampton Wanderers' deployment of the Harry J. Allstars' 'Liquidator'.

Chelsea were quickest on the uptake of the ska instrumental as walk-out music, with the sleeve notes to *Liquidator: The Best of the Harry J. Allstars* (2003) crediting the Blues' usage "way back in 1969" when it was first released. Wolves and the Baggies contest which of the West Midlands clubs used it first, although both temporarily ceased playing it under the instruction of the regional police, who controversially contended that both sets of fans' concocted lyrics incited violence.

Dennis Alcapone, a contemporary of Lee Perry, King Tubby and Prince Buster, had an alternative response to the rise of hooliganism and the racist ideologies of the National Front. And his riposte just so happened to reference one of West Brom's trailblazing trinity of black players — Cyrille Regis (born French Guiana), Laurie Cunningham (north London) and Brendon Batson (Grenada) — affectionately but patronisingly known as 'the Three Degrees' after the dark-skinned soul trio. Having relocated from Jamaica to London in 1974, Alcapone (real name Smith) wrote 'World Cup Football', offering some advice for Spain 1982:

> Thrills an' bubbles wasn't caused by troubles
> If you want to see some skill
> Come watch di team Brazil
> If England want to do somethin' good
> Hear me now, Ron Greenwood
> Forget your pride an' your prejudice
> And carry in di man Cyrille Regis
> Take out your little-little book
> And write down di name Garth Crooks

By the time the Reggae Boyz qualified for France '98, black players were no longer a rarity in British football, which is why the national team manager (Brazilian René Simões) combed the Premier League for players of Jamaican heritage. One of the forerunners to Earle, Barnes, Regis and Cunningham (who made history as both Real Madrid's first black and first British footballer), was Gilbert Saint Elmo Heron. Heron, nicknamed the Black Arrow, was born in

Jamaican capital Kingston and became Celtic's first black player in 1951. A distinguished achievement for sure, but if the name sounds familiar it's more likely owing to his son, Gil Scott-Heron, the soul-jazz musician and poet who insisted that 'The Revolution Will Not Be Televised' (1971) and is himself considered an influential forerunner to hip-hop.

Reviews

"It definitely was a term of endearment and I think there was an element of the *Cool Runnings* thing about it. But I thought it was slightly disrespectful. To be representing Jamaica on the world stage, I thought at times that it was a bit glib and bandied around a bit too much ... The Jamaican National Team, that's who we were. Whether we, or the Jamaican fans, wanted to call ourselves the Reggae Boyz was another thing. But I didn't like that everybody else was jumping on it."

– Robbie Earle speaking to *The Independent* in 2018 about the musical appellation first given to the team during a visit to Zambia in 1995

"What we are going to do with reggae music and with football is to capture France!"

– an excitable Horace Dalley, the Jamaican Junior Minister for Sports in 1998

"The 'Reggae Boyz anthem' was the collaborative effort dubbed 'Rise Up' ... What struck the world over was really the spirit of the Reggae Boyz and the support coming from Jamaica and the Caribbean at large."

– Biko Kennedy, 'Reggae on the Ball', jamaicansmusic.com (2013)

11. Waka Waka (This Time for Africa)

First released: 2010
Highest UK chart position: 21

The aural impact of the 2010 World Cup is manifested in the disparate shapes of the vuvuzela and Shakira.

To the elongated stadium horn first. The vuvuzela is technically categorised as a brass instrument, though they are commonly made from cheap injection-moulded plastic and many would question its categorisation as a musical instrument altogether. Freddie Maake, a fan of the Kaizer Chiefs (the South African football team, not the Yorkshire five-piece), claims to have fashioned the first vuvuzela from an aluminium bicycle horn in the mid-Sixties and to have coined its name from the Zulu words for 'welcome', 'unite' and 'celebration', although the Shembe, a religious group also known as the Nazareth Baptist Church, counterclaim that it's non-sporting origins can be traced back to the early 19th century and that football has stolen the power of their Holy Spirit. Affiliated with South Africa 2010, very similar devices are common in Latin America, although their approval is far from unanimous. The cacophony produced by thousands of horns blown in unison caused sound issues for broadcasters and critics also cited health and safety concerns, with demand for earplugs outstripping supply and a worry that they could be used as weapons. Like the old-fashioned rattle clacker before them, there were calls to ban vuvuzelas from stadiums. Uncharacteristically sensitive to local noise and colour, the residing FIFA President Sepp Blatter counselled against 'Europeanising' the first African World Cup, although South African news columnist Jon Qwelane argued in favour of a ban shortly after his country were selected as hosts, describing the vuvuzela as 'an instrument from hell'. Xabi Alonso was not a fan either; the Spain and Liverpool midfielder said after playing at the 2009 Confederations Cup rehearsal tournament, "That noise I don't like ... FIFA must ban those things." 'That noise' has been unflatteringly compared to a swarm of wasps and an elephant passing wind, and the offending instrument has been banned from subsequent World Cups, as well as from Wembley, Wimbledon, the Yankee Stadium and the Gabba Cricket Ground.

There were also no vuvuzelas to be seen or heard in 'Waka Waka (This Time for Africa)', the official FIFA song by Colombian songstress Shakira. The choice of performer stirred considerable controversy in the host nation, with proud Africans feeling slighted in favour of a Hispanic crossover star who appealed to the American and European mass markets. In hindsight, the choice of convicted sex offender R. Kelly, around whom accusations of exploitation and child abuse already swirled, to helm the official FIFA anthem 'Sign of a Victory' in conjunction with the Soweto Spiritual Singers should have proven more provocative. FIFA's distinction between song and anthem appears to be that the former is promotional while the latter serves a more ceremonial purpose, although both received a commercial release and appeared on *Listen Up! The Official 2010 FIFA World Cup Anthem*, which attempted to redress the complaints about African representation by also including songs in the indigenous languages of Fang, Duala and Xhosi. Long-term

World Cup sponsors Coca-Cola also came up with the diplomatic goods by selecting Somali-Canadian world music artist K'naan's 'Wavin' Flag' as a promotional anthem for the tournament's official fizzy drink.

In fairness to Shakira and her co-writer/producer John Hill, 'Waka Waka (This Time for Africa)' pays its dues to African culture, to such an extent that they were accused of plagiarism. To Western ears, the 'waka waka' refrain is dangerously close to rendering Shakira into a Fozzie Bear impersonator, yet for Afropop connoisseurs it was uncomfortably reminiscent of '*Zamina mina (Zangaléwa)*', a 1986 hit by Golden Sounds, a Cameroonian group specialising in the makossa style of urban music. The song was so popular that Golden Sounds, formed by active members of Cameroon's presidential guards, rebranded themselves Zangaléwa and its infectious rhythms traversed continents, enabled by the rise of music television and travelling DJs. It was also covered multiple times, including by Los Condes in Latin America, which could explain Shakira's familiarity with it, as could her Lebanese heritage. The name Shakira also means 'grateful' in Arabic, and she doubtless lived up to her name when an out-of-court settlement was reached and a press conference held in which band members Guy Dooh and Jean Paul Zé Bella and their manager Didier Edo sought to "enlighten international opinion" about Shakira's welcome adaptation. A lawsuit was also rumoured to be in the offing from Dominican musician Wilfrido Vargas, who in 1988 had rewritten '*Zangaléwa*' as '*El Negro No Puede*' (Blacks Cannot Sleep) for girl group Las Chicas del Can, although Vargas was quick to clarify that he wasn't the copyright owner. Indeed, Debora Halbert, author of *The State of Copyright: The Complex Relationships of Cultural Creation in a Globalized World* (2014) casts doubt on any claim to ownership by stating that the original chorus borrows from "military marches of unknown origins that go back as far as World War II". Fans of alternative rock can also hear it sampled in Vampire Weekend's cover of Bruce Springsteen's 'I'm Goin' Down'.

On the right side of art pop, Vampire Weekend are widely praised for their diverse influences, whereas fresh off mega-hits such as 'Hips Don't Lie' (with Wyclef Jean), 'Beautiful Liar' (with Beyoncé) and 'She Wolf', Shakira's blend of Congolese rumba guitar and Soca beats was widely seen as commercially derivative. She could draw on support, however, from Freshlyground, a local Afro-fusion band who were enlisted to inject further authenticity. Labelling themselves "the musical voice of a nation's adolescent democracy", Freshlyground were a mixture of black, white, male and female talent, fronted by lead vocalist Zolani Mahola. They wrote/performed a bridge and third verse and are given a 'featuring' credit on the single's sleeve, on which they form the black and white background to the colourful Shakira front and centre. Unlike some of their compatriots, they didn't begrudge her being headline act; violinist Kyla-Rose Smith shrewdly informed America's Public Broadcasting Service: "I think that the World Cup is a global event but it's also a business, a huge marketing exercise. FIFA requires a musician of a certain global reach to appeal to all the different kinds of people who are involved and witness and watch the World Cup. So I understand the choice of someone like Shakira."

Shifting more than ten million units worldwide, 'Waka Waka (This Time for Africa)' is the most commercially successful football song of all time. With a second-hand melody and lyrics surfing the same trite sport-as-battle analogy, sales can reasonably be attributed to the universal appeal held by Shakira's brand of high-energy pop. Music snobs might not think there's a great deal of competition for title of best World Cup Song but Ricky Martin's 'The Cup of Life' went to number one in 30 countries in 1998 and 'We Are One (Ole Ola)' by Pitbull featuring Jennifer Lopez and Claudia Leitte — sadly not an adaptation of Rod Stewart's Scottish samba — hit the top spot in 20 different locations in 2014. The occasionally discerning British public gave them all a lukewarm reception, perhaps due to the mild outbreak of xenophobia that tends to occur whenever our national interests are encroached upon — it seems to be damaging to the domestic self-esteem to acknowledge inferiority at football or pop. In France, Shakira held the number one position for six weeks and remained in the singles chart until 2013, totalling 132 weeks. In Germany, the song was also at number one for six weeks and was the second highest selling single of the year. And in Italy it spent a staggering 16 weeks at the top. It was also a number one in the great footballing nations of Argentina, Chile and Mexico, as well as Shakira's native Colombia. Its performance in the host country is harder to verify, since The Official South African Charts (TOSAC) was not established until 2021.

As with Martin's dual-language 'The Cup of Life'/'*La Copa de la Vida*', Shakira's bilingualism facilitated a Spanish-language version, 'Waka Waka (*Esto es África*)', which dominated the Spanish charts for 17 weeks, beating Italy by one, which is apt given that Spain supplanted the Azzurri as world champions in South Africa. Spain's tiki-taka tempo, conducted by midfield maestros Xavi and Andres Iniesta, mesmerised their opponents. Their club and international teammate, Barcelona defender Gerard Piqué, was similarly entranced by Shakira. The pair met on the set of the 'Waka Waka' music video — which sporadically cut to high-profile players exhibiting ball skills and/or merchandise clothing rather than joining in with the African tribal dance moves — and they embarked on a decade-long relationship that seemingly strengthened the rapport between music and football. Shakira and Piqué had two sons together, Milan and Sasha, but split in 2022. Very soon after, Piqué confirmed a new relationship with Clara Chía Martí, 12 years his junior, whereas Shakira was precisely ten years his senior (they share a birthday). Proving that football and music is not always a marriage made in heaven, the consequent diss track 'Music Sessions #53', in collaboration with Argentinian EDM and Latin trap DJ Bizarrap, took aim at Shakira's ex in their native tongue. Translated snippets include 'a she-wolf like me isn't for rookies ... I was out of your league' and 'I'm worth two 22-year-olds / You swapped a Ferrari for a [Renault] Twingo / You swapped a Rolex for a Casio'. The song set several Guinness World Records, including most streamed Latin track on Spotify in 24 hours (14,393,324) and most viewed Latin track on YouTube in the same time period (63 million).

The matadors who conquered South Africa might not have appreciated the discordant vuvuzela soundtrack, but Piqué probably wouldn't have objected to the contentious instrument drowning out his ex-partner's football-related follow-up with himself at the centre of its cracked heart.

Reviews

"Sonic vomit ... perhaps the stupidest official song for any major sporting event ever ... Red card for bad taste."

– Stuart Derdeyn, Postmedia Network Canada CD Reviews

"The lithe-limbed one's Official World Cup Song never quite dissolves into an all-out cheese-fest."

– Robert Copsey, Digital Spy

"Welds pretty, undulating African guitars to a clod-hopping, skippy township beat, with Shakira singing about an undisclosed event which is about to happen for Africa ... It could just as easily be about a global effort to build water-pipes in the worst drought-ridden areas of the continental land-mass as the World Cup."

– Fraser McAlpine, BBC Music

"A favourite of Nick Clegg, who shares [Shakira's] ability to wiggle from side to side."

– Dave Simpson, *The Guardian*

"One of the songs that the children are loving at the moment is Shakira, 'Waka Waka'. There's a lot of hip movements going along with a lot of dressing up. Charlotte particularly is running around the kitchen, in her dresses and ballet stuff. She goes completely crazy with Louis following her around trying to do the same thing."

– Prince William, President of the FA and future king, reveals his heirs' musical taste during an Apple audio walking tour recorded in December 2021

"Shakira's 2010 World Cup official song 'Waka Waka' has endured the test of time and remains a fútbol anthem today … [It] is a song you can't escape. And it'll go down in history as one of the most memorable World Cup songs."

– Griselda Flores, *Billboard* (2022)

12. Sweet Caroline

First released: 1969
Highest UK chart position: 8

When American soft rocker Neil Diamond wrote 'Sweet Caroline' for his second wife, little did he know that more than 50 years later there would be 80,000 England fans lustily reaching out...

Touching me,
Touching you ...
Sweet Caroline!

Mrs Diamond wasn't actually called Caroline, but her husband showed even more pragmatism than Gareth Southgate by taking his lyrical inspiration from the 11-year-old daughter of JFK and Jackie Onassis, a photo of whom happened to be on the cover of *Life* magazine, because her name fitted the melody better than Marcia.

'Sweet Caroline (Good Times Never Seemed So Good)', originally going by this elongated title, was recorded in Memphis, Tennessee and first released stateside in May 1969, where it charted at number four on the Billboard Hot 100. It didn't reach British shores until

February 1971, peaking at number eight on the UK charts, five places below Diamond's first overseas hit 'Cracklin' Rosie' three months before it. The song's sporting associations chart a similar transatlantic journey.

The Boston Red Sox were the first to play it regularly in a sports setting. Legend has it that in 1997 an employee of the Major League Baseball team gave birth to a baby girl named Caroline and the song was given a spin in her honour. Noting its crowd-pleasing qualities, the DJ at the Red Sox's Fenway Park stadium put it on rotation and the buoyancy of 'Sweet Caroline' made it something of a good luck charm. This was validated by Dr Charles Steinberg, who became executive vice president of public affairs at the Red Sox in 2002 and promptly made it a more ritualistic element of game day. "The song may have transformative powers," he reasoned. It has been played in the middle of the penultimate eighth inning at every game since and has spurred the Red Sox on to four World Series championships in the past 20 years, breaking a 75-year drought. Following the Boston Marathon bombing in April 2013, Diamond made a surprise appearance at Fenway Park to lead the crowd in a life-affirming rendition, which made it a city-wide anthem of solidarity. Downloads surged and the philanthropic singer-songwriter pledged all future royalties from 'Sweet Caroline' to the One Fund Boston charity set up to support those affected by the bombing, so casualties are benefiting from its spread to other sports.

The NFL's Carolina Panthers have also been playing the song, for fairly obvious reasons, since the turn of the century, and in the first decade of the new millennium it was taken up by the University of Pittsburgh and Pennsylvania State University as a rallying anthem for multi-sport events, although Pennsylvania temporarily abandoned it due to concerns about the lyrical content in the wake of a child sex scandal engulfing the Penn State Nittany Lions American football team. In the boxing arena, Tyson Fury has been known to belt out hits such as 'American Pie' and 'Walking in Memphis', and in November 2022 the 'Gypsy King' released his own version of 'Sweet Caroline', with proceeds going to Talk Club, a men's mental health charity. When played to the crowd ahead of his world-title defence against Derek Chisora the following month, 70,000 spectators at the Tottenham Hotspur Stadium provided rapturous accompaniment. The same stadium reverberated to the same song when Anthony Joshua lost his heavyweight title to Oleksandr Usyk in September 2021.

UK boxing, however, was filching from UK football, which had already embraced 'Sweet Caroline'. 'Where it began, I can't begin to know when' goes the opening line, but Northern Ireland fans contest that it can be dated back to Windsor Park, 7 September 2005, when Lawrie Sanchez's Green and White Army defeated England 1-0 in a World Cup qualifier and they sang in delight, making it all the more galling that the beaten side now claim it as their own. Gary McAllister, chairman of the Amalgamation of Official Northern Ireland Supporters' Clubs, demurred during Euro 2020:

> "I don't know how any England supporter can say they didn't know it was a Northern Ireland song. I would have thought that the sound of 'Sweet Caroline' was still ringing in their ears from September 2005 because it was extremely loud that night."

The tug of war definitely leans in favour of football and Ulster over boxing and England; Eddie Hearn could claim to have introduced 'Caroline' to Matchroom Sports boxing cards before it became popular at Wembley, but the routine practice of playing Neil Diamond before the main event appears to have been influenced by the song's enthusiastic uptake at the bouts of Belfast super-bantamweight Carl Frampton, who won his first amateur title the same year that Northern Ireland gave the mighty England a bloody nose and would go on to fight for world titles in New York and Las Vegas, with travelling fans returning the tune back across the Atlantic.

'Sweet Caroline' had also been on a tour of UK football grounds between Windsor Park and Wembley. When Reading made their first appearance in the top tier of English football in the 2006-07 season, it was played at the players' request. Glen Little, who made his first senior appearance on loan at Derry City a decade before Rooney, Beckham and Owen were embarrassed on Irish turf, revealed that a group of Reading players who referred to themselves as the Magnificent Seven had been celebrating their record Championship points total at an Indian restaurant in Marbella when "we just started singing it, everyone joined in and we actually ended up getting kicked out for being a bit too noisy!" The song petered out at the Madejski Stadium and then, a decade on, a Reading fan named Fran contacted BBC Radio Berkshire to discuss how to whip up a better atmosphere at home matches. Little responded with the suggestion that they bring back 'Sweet Caroline', which they did, and this time it stuck, although in a later meeting between club representatives and the Supporters Trust at Reading (STAR) it was mooted that the warm-up music was in need of a refresh, with one alternative being an offer from local band the Amazons to write a new club song, following on from earlier efforts by commercial director Kevin Girdler ('The Royals Anthem', 1991) and co-chairwoman Lady Khunying Sasima Svrikorn ('They Call Us the Royals', 2015).

Aston Villa latched onto the song after snatching a draw at Stoke in 2019. The Britannia Stadium speakers blasted out 'Sweet Caroline' after the final whistle and the Villa fans took it with them on a 12-match unbeaten run that catapulted them to the Championship play-offs, a penalty shoot-out victory over local rivals West Brom and eventual promotion to the Premier League. The following season, when they scraped Premier League survival with a final-day draw at West Ham, a video of the squad celebrating to the strains of 'Sweet Caroline' in the London Stadium dressing room prompted a response from the world's most famous Villan, Prince William, who retweeted from the official Kensington Palace Twitter account, "Never in doubt 😬 #UpTheVilla W".

The song has also been heard regularly at Arsenal's Emirates Stadium and Chelsea's Stamford Bridge, although some overstimulated Blues fans caused offence when taking the song back to Windsor Park for the UEFA Super Cup against Villarreal in August 2021 and adding the words 'F*** the Pope' into the three beats between the euphoric title shout and 'Good times never seemed so good'.

Just a few weeks prior to this egregious maltreatment of Diamond's chorus, the 'good times never seemed so good' lyrics resonated with a Wembley crowd who'd been starved of live entertainment throughout the COVID-19 lockdowns. Football and music were just two of the casualties of coronavirus, with no touching of hands permitted unless you were the amorous Health Secretary and his aide. Euro 2020 was pushed back to the summer of 2021 and even then it had to take place under social distancing restrictions. Wembley was at less than half capacity for the round-of-16 match between England and Germany. The Three Lions had needed to top their group to retain home advantage in a tournament split between 11 host nations, in a pan-European format that was supposed to celebrate the championship's 60th anniversary but proved a logistical nightmare in the midst of a global pandemic. People had become so delirious that Scotland's Tartan Army had even started warbling 'Yes Sir, I Can Boogie', a 1977 holiday hit by Spanish duo Baccara, which was an in-joke involving Aberdeen defender Andrew Considine's stag-do shenanigans being recreated (and shared via social media) when Scotland ended more than 20 years of hurt by beating Serbia to qualify for their first major tournament in a generation.

At Wembley, England were about to beat Germany in knockout football for the first time since 1966. The pre-chorus build to 'Sweet Caroline' perfectly mirrored the tone of anticipation and, when it was played before kick-off, TV pundits commented on the febrile atmosphere the song generated. Its potency had first been revealed to stadium DJ Tony Perry pre-pandemic, when the New York Yankees and Boston Red Sox converged on the former Olympic Stadium in east London for the 2019 Major League Baseball London Series. With the Red Sox designated the 'home' team, 'Sweet Caroline' rang out in the middle of the eighth and Perry has since told the *New York Times*, "That's where I picked up on those special powers."

'Three Lions' was the go-to track at the end of the 90 minutes. To follow, Perry hovered over the traditional 'Vindaloo' before opting for 'Sweet Caroline'. He told TalkSport he "went with [his] gut", backed by the match director telling him via an in-ear monitor, "The world's been closed for 18 months ... let 'em have it". The players who were still out applauding the support joined arms and joined in, as did those in the stands. As if to prove the song's unifying force, Perry maintains that "even the German fans were belting it out in the end", while Neil Diamond impersonators sprang up in households across the country. 'Three Lions' co-writer Frank Skinner had to concede, "I thought 'Sweet Caroline' went slightly better than 'Three Lions' in the post-match sing-song. I felt like we'd beat Germany and lost to Neil Diamond in extra time."

The scenes were repeated in the quarter-final and semi-final victories over Ukraine and Denmark respectively. 'Sweet Caroline' looked like being a good luck charm for the English national side. Unfortunately it wasn't enough to carry the men all the way to glory, though Italy's penalty shoot-out victory was perhaps karma for the mindlessness of fans whose antisocial behaviour at the final resulted in England playing behind closed doors again.

The song's talismanic qualities instead passed to the women. Getting in on the act during Euro 2022, a Dingbats-style billboard for Sainsbury's pictured a swede, carrot and lime and asked us to "Sing it for the Lionesses"! There were no Carolines in that history-making squad, but the alliterative Chloe Kelly was the next best thing, and her championship-winning goal against Germany gave her the last word. Or rather, she borrowed the last words from Neil Diamond, running off with the BBC microphone mid-interview to join her teammates and a record women's football crowd of 77,768 in a rousing chorus of 'Sweet Caroline'.

Reviews

"It's a song to celebrate good things, and it seems to bring good luck to those who embrace it."

– Neil Diamond himself

"You can't beat a bit of Neil Diamond. It's just a really joyous song, I think, that brings people together."

– Gareth Southgate

"The Diamond appeal is that he doesn't overcomplicate anything. That very simple sing-along chorus just makes it perfect, and everyone knows it."

– Steve Furst, Neil Diamond tribute act

"We had it first!"

– Northern Irish broadcaster Eamon Holmes

Acknowledgements

As with pop songs and football tactics, originality is an illusion — we are all building on what's gone before. I am indebted to the multitude of writers, researchers, historians and academics, not to mention musicians and footballers, who've already tackled this subject — consider this a compilation, a 'best of' all the pre-existing material, hopefully with my own input taking it in new directions.

A quick word on the reams of material that had to be omitted — the long-lost track 'We Were There' for example, performed by England's 1966 World Cup winners and intended to rival the 1982 squad's 'This Time We'll Get It Right' but shelved due to Falkland War sensitivities. And apologies for not finding space until now for Birkenhead surrealists Half Man Half Biscuit, who once turned down an appearance on Channel 4 music show *The Tube* because their beloved Tranmere Rovers were at home that night, but whose extensive football oeuvre ('The Referee's Alphabet', 'All I Want for Christmas is a Dukla Prague Away Kit', 'Bob Wilson: Anchorman') is more alternative than anthemic. They are worth checking out in their own right, as are Colin Irwin's *Sing When You're Winning* and Andrew Lawn's *We Lose Every Week*, especially if this book has done anything to pique your interest in the stories and the sociology behind chants rather than records. Special mention too to footballandmusic.co.uk, which is a treasure trove of mostly useless information that will nevertheless have you disappearing down rabbit holes of audiovisual 'delights'.

Thanks to Rob and Adam at Halcyon Publishing for seeing the potential in the concept, guiding me through the publishing process and finessing the end product. And thanks to Steve for taking my amateurish cover design and coming up with something a lot better!

Big thanks to all those stakeholders who bothered to provide exclusive 'reviews', in particular those who went above and beyond such as Marching Out Together's Andrew and the Astle family — it was a pleasure to learn about Laraine's crush on Bobby Moore as well as her fond memories of Jeff and 'Back Home'.

Last but certainly not least, thank you to the friends and family who contributed in various ways, from lending specific club expertise to providing proofreading services (Paul Martins on the football/music side, Marie and Penny on the SPaG side). This was not a solo effort and the author would be nothing without his assist makers or backing singers.

By the same author

Fortune's Always Hiding: From Stratford to Seville (2023)

Inside the Academy: The Hopes, Highs and Heartbreaks of West Ham United's Youth (2024)

Selected bibliography

'Back Home 50 years on', *Morning Star Online*, 18 April 2020

Blue Day — Wembley '97: The Heroes' Stories, Richard Godden, Trinity Mirror Sport Media, 2017

'Blue is still the Colour! Celebrating 50 years since the release of Chelsea's iconic anthem', *chelseafc.com*, 16 February 2022

Cockney Reject, Jeff Turner, John Blake Publishing, 2005

'From Männer in Rot to the Norwich City Calypso: The joy of football 7" singles', Pascal Claude, *When Saturday Comes*, January 2020

Get It On: How the '70s Rocked Football, Jon Spurling, Biteback Publishing, 2022

'Gerry Marsden: Why YNWA is special to me', Steve Hunter, *liverpoolfc.com*, 31 October 2013

'It's Coming Home: The history of the England fan chant', Joe Sommerlad, *The Independent*, 7 July 2021

Liverpool — Wondrous Place: Music from Cavern to Cream, Paul Du Noyer, Virgin Books, 2002

'Ossie's Dream', *Morning Star Online*, 23 April 2021

Ossie's Dream: My Autobiography, Ossie Ardiles, Bantam Press, 2009

'Remember BBC's Italia 90 opening credits? Here's the incredible story behind them', Ryan Bailey, *The 42*, 16 June 2015

Sing When You're Winning: Football Fans, Terrace Songs and a Search for the Soul of Soccer, Colin Irwin, André Deutsch, 2006

Sport, Music, Identities, Anthony Bateman (ed.), Routledge, 2015

"'The Butter-Cup that Blooms in Spring': Crowd Singing on the Eve of the First World War', Paul Newsham, *Playing Pasts*, 1 May 2022

The People's Songs: The Story of Modern Britain in 50 Records, Stuart Maconie, Ebury Press, 2013

'The Science Behind Singing: What Happens When We Sing?', Stefan Joubert, *London Singing Institute*, 1 February 2020

The Soccer Tribe, Desmond Morris, Jonathan Cape, 1981

'The story of Bubbles', John Helliar, *whufc.com*, 17 October 2007

'Wales: So "Cool Cymru" Part I', Iain Ellis, *Pop Matters*, 27 July 2010

'Was Liverpool the Home of the Singing Sixties?', Simon Hart, *The Independent*, 26 February 2012

We Lose Every Week: The History of Football Chanting, Andrew Lawn, Ockley Books, 2020

'When — and why — did Everton FC and Liverpool FC fans start singing at matches?', Paddy Shennan, *The Liverpool Echo*, 4 October 2011

'Why New Order's football song 'World in Motion' was a game-changer', Nick Hasted, *The Independent*, 13 June 2018

'World In Motion: the making of the greatest World Cup song', Mark Russell, *GQ*, 15 June 2018

'You'll Never Walk Alone: A Powerful Song for Troubled Times', Martin Chilton, *Dig!*, 6 December 2020

"'You'll Never Walk Alone' Is Our Song!', *Manchester Evening News*, 19 February 2007

1966 and Not All That, Mark Perryman (ed.), Repeater Books, 2016

'50 years after its premiere, the stories behind The Rock of the World Cup', Claudio Vergara, *Latercera*, 4 July 2018